AF596531

# Ancient Rome for Beginners

*The Story of the Roman Empire Simplified for People Who Slept Through History Class*

# Free Bonus from Captivating History (Available for a Limited time)

Hi History Lovers!

Now you have a chance to join our exclusive history list so you can get your first history ebook for free as well as discounts and a potential to get more history books for free!

Simply visit the link below to join.

captivatinghistory.com/ebook

Or, Scan the QR code!

Also, make sure to follow us on Facebook, X, and YouTube by searching for Captivating History.

# Table of Contents

# Introduction

You've probably never given much thought to ancient Rome. Maybe you dozed off during that one history class where the teacher droned on about togas and aqueducts. Maybe you watched *Gladiator* and thought, "Cool fight scenes," then moved on with your life. Or maybe you've simply never had a reason to care about a civilization that collapsed over 1,500 years ago.

But here's the thing: Rome never really left.

Right now, as you're reading this, you're surrounded by Roman ghosts. The alphabet on this page? Thank the Romans, who adapted it from the Greeks and Etruscans and spread it across Europe. The language itself—if you're reading in English, French, Spanish, Italian, or Portuguese—is packed with Latin roots. Estimates suggest that roughly 60 percent of English words derive from Latin, either directly or filtered through French after the Norman Conquest. When you say "calculate" or "sincere" or "legal," you're actually speaking a language that would sound familiar to a Roman scholar.

Look around your city. See that government building with the columns and the dome? That's Roman architecture. The US Capitol building is basically a love letter to Roman design. So is the Panthéon in Paris, the British Museum in London, and thousands of other structures across the Western world. For centuries, if you wanted a building to look important and authoritative, you made it look Roman.

The laws that govern your life have Roman DNA, though the degree varies depending on where you live. If you're in a country with a civil law system, like France, Germany, Italy, or most of Latin America, your legal code descends directly from Roman law through the *Corpus Juris Civilis* compiled under Emperor Justinian. If you're in a common-law country like the United States or the United Kingdom, the connection is less direct but still present. The concept that defendants should be presumed innocent, a cornerstone of modern justice, has roots in Roman legal thought, though the modern principle was developed later. Legal terms like "subpoena," "habeas corpus," and "pro bono" are straight-up Latin because our entire legal vocabulary evolved from Roman frameworks.

Your calendar is Roman. July is named after Julius Caesar. August is named after Augustus, Rome's first emperor. The structure you use (12 months, 365 days, with leap years) comes from the Julian calendar reform of 45 BCE, when Caesar fixed Rome's chaotic old calendar that had gotten wildly out of sync with the seasons. Before that reform, Roman priests had to insert extra months whenever they felt like it just to keep things aligned.

Even your entertainment echoes Roman spectacle. The Romans didn't invent the human appetite for watching dramatic conflict and competition, but they perfected it on a massive scale. They packed fifty thousand people into the Colosseum to watch gladiators battle, exotic animals get slaughtered, and criminals get executed in elaborate theatrical productions. They understood that crowds would gather to watch spectacles and violence and that the state could use those gatherings for political purposes. The medium has changed, but the appetite for public competition and drama hasn't.

Christianity, whether you practice it or not, shaped Western civilization in ways that are impossible to untangle from Roman history. Jesus was born in a Roman province and executed by Roman authorities. His followers spread their message along Roman roads, and they were protected (and sometimes persecuted) by Roman law. Christianity was legalized in 313 CE under Constantine and then became the official state religion in 380 under Emperor Theodosius I. When Christianity became part of the empire, it inherited organizational structures, administrative divisions, and political thinking that still shape the Catholic Church today. The Catholic Church's hierarchy, with its pope in Rome and its administrative territories, reflects the Roman world in which it grew up. Even the word "cardinal" comes from the Latin *cardo*, meaning "hinge."

The point is that Rome isn't dead. It's a fossil that turned into the bedrock beneath modern Western civilization. You can't understand how

Europe became Europe, how America became America, or how the Western world developed its ideas about government, law, military organization, engineering, and culture without understanding ancient Rome.

But here's what makes Rome truly fascinating. It was a spectacular mess that somehow worked for over a thousand years. This wasn't a civilization that ran smoothly under wise and benevolent rulers. Ancient Rome could be chaotic, brutal, corrupt, innovative, and astonishingly resilient. It was built by fratricide (according to legend), grew through near-constant warfare, survived multiple civil wars, endured insane emperors and plagues, and yet somehow managed to control most of Europe, North Africa, and the Middle East for centuries.

Rome started as a muddy village on the Tiber River—a backwater settlement that no one would have bet on. It grew into a republic where citizens (well, some citizens) had a voice in government. Then it transformed into an empire ruled by emperors who ranged from brilliant administrators to raving lunatics. It built the largest road network the world had ever seen, created concrete that still stands today, and developed military tactics that armies studied for the next two thousand years. It also enslaved millions, destroyed entire civilizations, and committed atrocities that would make modern war criminals blush.

This book is going to take you through the entire story—all 1,200 years of it. We're starting in 753 BCE with the legendary founding of Rome and ending in 476 CE, when the last Western Roman emperor was quietly deposed. We'll cover the rise of the Roman Republic, the Punic Wars against Carthage, the assassination of Julius Caesar, daily life in ancient Rome, and the slow collapse that historians call "the fall of Rome" (though it was more complicated than a simple fall).

Here's the timeline in broad strokes:

**753-509 BCE: The Monarchy.** Rome is supposedly ruled by seven kings, starting with Romulus (who almost certainly didn't exist as described in legend) and ending with Tarquin the Proud (who might have been a real person, though the stories about him are likely exaggerated). The historical truth is murky. Archaeology tells us Rome existed at this time, but the tales of these early kings blend myth and propaganda. What we do know is that by 509 BCE, Rome had kicked out its last king and developed a permanent hatred of the monarchy.

**509–27 BCE: The Republic.** Rome develops a complex system of government with elected consuls, a Senate, and citizen assemblies. This is the era of Roman expansion, the Punic Wars, and the rise of powerful generals like Marius, Sulla, Pompey, and Julius Caesar. The Roman Republic ends in civil war and Caesar's assassination.

**27 BCE–180 CE: The Early Empire and the Golden Age.** Augustus becomes the first emperor while pretending he isn't. Rome enjoys the Pax Romana, two hundred years of relative peace and prosperity. This is when Rome reaches its greatest territorial extent and builds most of the monuments we associate with Rome. It's also when you see some truly insane emperors like Caligula and Nero.

**180–284 CE: The Crisis Years.** Things start falling apart. The empire faces civil wars, economic collapse, plague, and pressure from outside invaders. In a fifty-year period, Rome has over twenty different emperors, most of whom die violently.

**284–476 CE: The Late Empire and the Fall.** Diocletian splits the empire into eastern and western halves to make it easier to govern. Constantine legalizes Christianity and moves the capital to Constantinople. Barbarian tribes push into Roman territory. In 476 CE, a Germanic chieftain named Odoacer deposed the last Western Roman emperor, a teenager named Romulus Augustulus, and the Western Roman Empire effectively ended. (The Eastern Empire, later called the Byzantine Empire, continued for another thousand years, but that's a different story.)

This book seeks to explain ancient Rome in a way that makes sense to people who know nothing about it. We're not going to go into obscure debates that only concern academics. We're not going to skip over the interesting parts to focus on dry details about specific laws. And we're definitely not going to assume you remember anything from high school history class.

What we are going to do is tell the story of how a small city on a river became the most powerful empire in the Western world, how it maintained that power for centuries, and why it eventually collapsed. We'll explain how the Roman government worked, how Roman soldiers fought, what daily life was actually like, and why the Romans did some of the bizarre things they did (like watching people get killed for entertainment or worshipping their emperors as gods).

Let's start at the beginning, in that muddy village where legend says two brothers raised by a wolf decided to build a city. One of them ended up

dead. The other became Rome's first king. It's a fitting beginning for an empire built on violence, ambition, and an unshakeable belief that Rome was destined to rule the world.

# Chapter 1: From Wolf-Milk to Mud Huts

## Myth vs. Reality: Romulus, Remus, and the Fratricide That Started It All

Every great civilization needs an origin story, and Rome's is a doozy. According to legend, it all began in 753 BCE with twin brothers, a she-wolf, and a murder.

The story goes like this. A princess named Rhea Silvia was forced to become a Vestal Virgin, which meant she had to remain celibate for at least thirty years. According to the legend, this was to prevent her from having children who might challenge her uncle's throne. But the god Mars had other plans. He seduced (or assaulted, depending on which version you read) Rhea Silvia, and she gave birth to twin boys named Romulus and Remus.

In the traditional account, her uncle ordered the infants thrown into the Tiber River. The servant tasked with this job could not quite bring himself to drown two babies, so he left them in a basket near the riverbank, hoping nature would do the dirty work for him.

Instead, a she-wolf found the twins and nursed them. Yes, the boys grew up on wolf milk. The boys survived and were eventually discovered by a shepherd named Faustulus. They grew up strong and ambitious. When they learned their true heritage, they killed their uncle and decided to found a city of their own.

The she-wolf nursing Remus and Romulus.[1]

This is where things got messy. The brothers could not agree on where to build their city or who would rule it. Romulus wanted Palatine Hill. Remus preferred Aventine Hill. They decided to let the gods choose by watching for birds, a practice called augury that the ancient Romans would use for centuries to make important decisions. In the most common version of the story, Romulus claimed to see twelve vultures while Remus saw only six. In another version, Remus saw his six birds first, but Romulus saw more in total. Either way, the sources agree that a dispute followed, and Romulus declared victory.

Remus, being a sore loser, mocked his brother by jumping over the incomplete city walls, saying, "These walls are pathetic. Anyone could breach them." Romulus responded by killing him on the spot, allegedly declaring, "So perish anyone else who leaps over my walls."

And that's how Rome was founded. According to tradition, Romulus became the first king. He ruled for thirty-seven years before mysteriously vanishing during a thunderstorm and supposedly ascending to become a god.

It's a great story. It's also almost certainly fiction.

Archaeology tells a different tale. The area that would become Rome was inhabited long before 753 BCE. Evidence shows scattered settlements on Rome's hills dating back to at least 1000 BCE. These were not organized cities, just small villages of farmers and shepherds living in simple huts. Around 800 to 750 BCE, these villages started merging into a larger settlement. The famous seven hills of Rome—Palatine, Aventine, Capitoline, Quirinal, Viminal, Esquiline, and Caelian—each had its own communities that gradually unified.

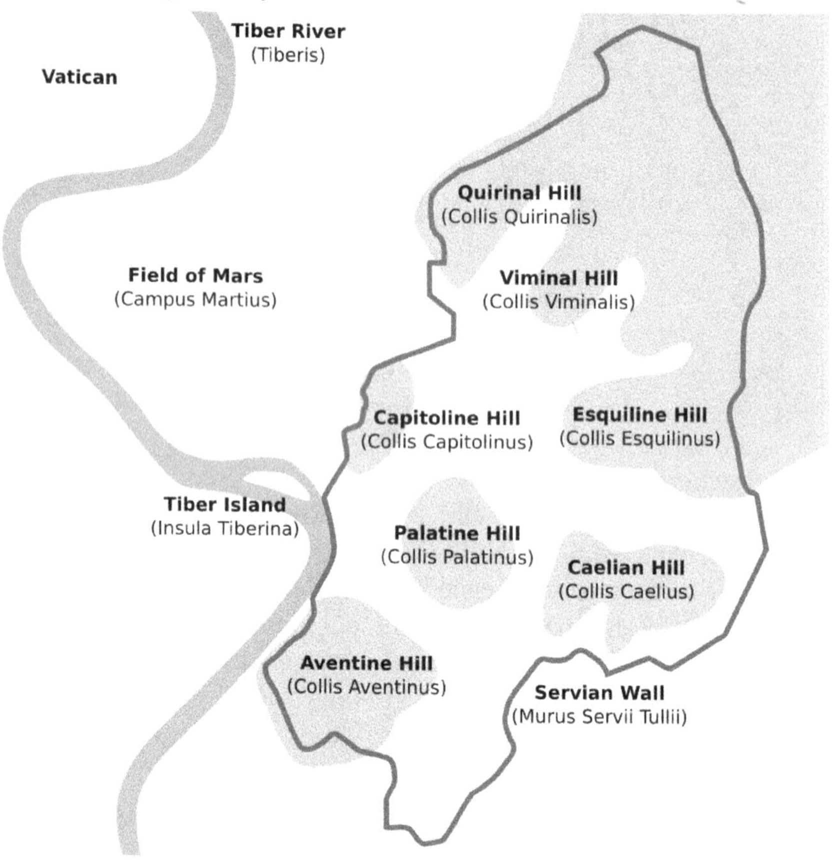


**The seven hills of Rome.**[3]

The process was likely messy, slow, and boring. There were no divine twins. No she-wolf. Just people deciding that cooperation offered better protection and trade opportunities than staying isolated. The Romans later developed the Romulus story, drawing on Greek models and older Italic traditions to give their city a mythical pedigree that could rival the legendary foundations of Greek cities like Athens or Thebes.

The Romans themselves, at least some of them, likely knew their foundation myth was propaganda. Ancient historians like Livy admitted they could not verify the early stories. Yet they kept telling them anyway because the myths served a purpose. They explained why Rome was special and why Romans had a divine mandate to conquer. The story justified centuries of expansion and war.

So when we talk about Rome's founding, we are really talking about two things: the myth that Romans told themselves and the archaeological reality of a settlement growing on some hills next to a river. Both versions matter. The myth shaped the Roman identity. The reality shaped their circumstances.

What was early Rome actually like? Archaeological excavations on Palatine Hill have uncovered post holes and debris from 8th-century BCE huts, simple oval structures with wattle-and-daub walls and thatched roofs. These were not impressive buildings. A typical hut was maybe ten to fifteen feet across, housing an entire family plus their few possessions. The floor was made of dirt. Cooking happened over an open fire that also provided heat and light. Most Romans were farmers who grew grain, kept a few animals, and hoped nothing went wrong.

The location mattered more than the buildings. Rome sat at one of the most practical crossing points of the Tiber River, about fifteen miles from the sea, with Tiber Island providing natural stepping stones. This made it a natural trade hub where goods moving between Etruria in the north and the Greek colonies in the south had to pass through. The hills provided defense, as it was harder to attack people there than on a flat plain. The river provided water, fish, and transportation. The surrounding land was fertile enough to support farming.

Early Rome survived because of its position and its ability to absorb outsiders. The Romans were never ethnically pure; they were a mix of Latins, Sabines, Etruscans, and whoever else showed up and proved useful. This openness to incorporating foreigners would become one of Rome's greatest strengths. Other cities jealously guarded citizenship. Rome eventually gave it to half the Mediterranean world.

### The Seven Kings: How Rome Began as a Monarchy (and Why They Eventually Hated Kings)

According to Roman tradition, Rome was ruled by seven kings between 753 and 509 BCE. The list is suspiciously neat. Exactly seven rulers over exactly 244 years? Most historians think this chronology was tidied up later to make Rome's early history sound more organized than it actually was.

Still, the stories of these kings, even if partially invented, reveal what the ancient Romans believed about their own past.

Romulus (r. 753–716 BCE) was the legendary founder who supposedly established Rome's first institutions. He created the Senate, a council of elders who advised the king. He also solved Rome's woman problem—the new city had plenty of men but few women—by inviting the neighboring Sabines to a festival and then having Roman men abduct the Sabine women. This event, called the Rape of the Sabines, was later depicted in countless paintings and sculptures as if kidnapping your neighbors' daughters was a romantic way to start a civilization. The Sabines naturally declared war, but eventually, the stolen women intervened and negotiated peace. The two peoples merged, doubling Rome's population.

**Abduction of a Sabine Woman by Giambologna.**[8]

Numa Pompilius (r. 715-673 BCE) was supposedly the complete opposite of Romulus. He was peaceful, religious, and obsessed with proper rituals. He allegedly created Rome's religious calendar, established the Vestal Virgins (priestesses who maintained Rome's sacred flame dedicated to Vesta, the Roman goddess of the hearth and home), and built temples to various gods. If Romulus was the warrior founder, Numa was the priest-king who gave Rome its spiritual structure. He claimed to get advice from a water nymph named Egeria, which was convenient when he needed divine justification for his decisions.

Tullus Hostilius (r. 673-642 BCE) swung back toward warfare. His name literally means "hostile," which tells you something about his reputation. He conquered nearby Alba Longa after a bizarre ritual combat in which three brothers from each side fought to the death (Rome's team won). He allegedly died when Jupiter, the chief Roman god, struck his house with lightning. Ancient Romans interpreted this as divine punishment for performing a religious ritual incorrectly.

Ancus Marcius (r. 642-617 BCE) was supposedly Numa's grandson and tried to balance warfare with religious devotion. He expanded Rome's territory, built the first bridge across the Tiber, and founded the port city of Ostia at the river's mouth, giving Rome access to sea trade. He probably was not a real person, but the bridge and the port certainly existed, so someone built them.

Here is where things get more historically solid. The last three kings were Etruscans, members of a more advanced civilization north of Rome that had a profound influence on Roman culture.

Tarquinius Priscus (r. 616-579 BCE), also called Tarquin the Elder, was supposedly the son of a Greek merchant who moved to Rome and impressed everyone with his wealth and ambition. He gained the kingship through a process involving approval from the Senate and assemblies. This was not a popular election in the modern sense; it was more like acceptance by Rome's leading families. Tarquin the Elder launched major building projects. He started draining the swampy valley between Rome's hills, creating what would become the Forum, Rome's central meeting place. He also began building the Temple of Jupiter Optimus Maximus on Capitoline Hill, which would become Rome's most important religious site.

The Forum of Rome today.[4]

Servius Tullius (r. 578–535 BCE) was credited with organizing Roman society into classes based on wealth and military service. The "Servian constitution" divided citizens into groups according to how much property they owned, which determined what military equipment they could afford and thus what role they would play in the army. Richer citizens formed the cavalry and heavy infantry. Poorer citizens served as light troops. The poorest served as rowers in the navy or did not serve at all. This system of connecting wealth to military obligation would define Roman society for centuries.

Servius also supposedly built Rome's first defensive wall. The Servian Wall that visitors can see today near Rome's Termini Station was actually constructed in the 4th century BCE, after the Gallic sack of 390 BCE, though it might have followed the line of an earlier fortification. Servius expanded the city to include all seven hills and organized it into administrative districts. He was murdered by his son-in-law, Tarquin the Proud, who wanted the throne for himself.

Tarquinius Superbus (r. 535–509 BCE), better known as Tarquin the Proud, was Rome's last king and the villain of the story. According to tradition, he seized power through violence, ruled as a tyrant without consulting the Senate, and generally behaved like a king in a cautionary tale about why monarchy is bad.

The stories about Tarquin emphasize his cruelty and arrogance. He supposedly maintained power through fear and violence, executing political opponents and confiscating their property. His sons were equally terrible. One of them, Sextus Tarquinius, allegedly raped Lucretia, the wife of a Roman nobleman. Lucretia told her husband and father what happened, made them swear to avenge her, and then stabbed herself to death rather than live with the shame.

Her rape and suicide sparked a revolution. A nobleman named Lucius Junius Brutus rallied support, and the Romans expelled Tarquin and his entire family from the city. They swore never to have another king again. The year was 509 BCE.

How much of this is true? Some of it likely is. Tarquin the Proud likely existed, as his name appears in sources outside Rome. The Etruscans probably did rule Rome for a period. The revolution probably happened, though perhaps not as dramatically as the story suggests. However, Lucretia's suicide reads more like a morality play than history, a story Romans told to justify their hatred of kings and to celebrate the virtues of female honor and male vengeance.

The main thing is that Rome transitioned from a monarchy to a republic around 509 BCE, probably through a combination of internal revolts and external pressure from other Latin cities. The Romans later dramatized this transition into a founding myth for their republic, just as they had mythologized their city's original founding.

## The Etruscan Influence: The Neighbors Who Shaped Rome

If you want to truly understand early Rome, you need to understand the Etruscans. They were the sophisticated neighbors who profoundly shaped Roman culture in ways that lasted for centuries, yet they remain mysterious because most of their writings have not survived.

The Etruscans lived in Etruria (modern Tuscany) north of Rome. By 800 BCE, while Rome was still a collection of mud huts, Etruscan cities like Veii, Tarquinia, and Caere were thriving urban centers with stone temples, elaborate tombs, sophisticated metalwork, and long-distance trade networks. They dealt in Greek pottery, worked bronze and iron, and had a written language adapted from the Greek alphabet.

Etruscan culture influenced Rome in practical ways. The Romans borrowed Etruscan engineering, learning to drain swamps, build arches, and construct stone foundations for temples. The famous Roman gladiatorial games likely developed from Etruscan funeral rites, though some scholars point to Campanian origins. The purple-bordered toga that Roman magistrates wore was part of the Etruscan fashion. The bundle of rods and axes (called *fasces*) that symbolized Roman authority was an Etruscan symbol of power.

Even the Roman alphabet came through the Etruscans, who had adapted it from Greek colonists in southern Italy. Etruscan religious practices, such as reading omens from bird flight, examining animal entrails to predict the future, and interpreting lightning strikes, became core Roman religious rituals. The Romans never felt confident making major decisions without checking for divine approval, and the Etruscans taught them how.

The Etruscans also likely introduced Greek culture to Rome. Greek colonies dotted southern Italy and Sicily, but Rome had limited direct contact with them early on. The Etruscans, who traded extensively with the Greeks, served as cultural middlemen. Through them, Romans encountered Greek art, mythology, and architecture. Many Roman gods were basically Greek gods with Latin names. Jupiter was Zeus, Venus was Aphrodite, and Neptune was Poseidon. This syncretism probably happened through Etruscan influence.

**An Etruscan painting of dancers and musicians.**[5]

Politically, the Etruscans might have taught Rome how to organize a city-state. Etruscan cities had kings, councils, and citizen assemblies. They had laws and social hierarchies. Rome's governmental structure during the monarchy period looks suspiciously similar to Etruscan models.

The relationship between the early Romans and the Etruscans was complicated. Sometimes they traded. Sometimes they fought. The three Etruscan kings who ruled Rome showed that Etruscans could gain power in the city, but their eventual expulsion also showed Roman resentment of foreign rule. After the republic was established, Rome spent the next few centuries conquering the Etruscan cities one by one.

By 300 BCE, Etruscan power had been largely broken. By 100 BCE, the Etruscan language was dying out as people adopted Latin. By the time of the Roman Empire, Etruria was just another region of Italy. The Etruscans vanished as a distinct culture, but their influence remained embedded in Roman civilization, including in their DNA.

Modern archaeology has revealed Etruscan cities, tombs filled with elaborate frescoes and grave goods, and enough inscriptions to partially understand their language. However, we cannot read most Etruscan literature because it did not survive. The Romans absorbed Etruscan culture but did not preserve Etruscan writings. What we know about the Etruscans comes largely from their artwork, their tombs, and what the Romans bothered to record about them.

It is one of history's ironies. The people who civilized Rome are now remembered primarily through Roman sources, many of which were written centuries after the Etruscan culture had faded. The teachers became footnotes in the students' story.

## The Birth of the Republic: The Scandal That Ended the Monarchy

The transition from monarchy to republic changed everything about how Rome functioned, even if it took time for those changes to fully develop.

When the Romans expelled Tarquin the Proud in 509 BCE, they did not get rid of just one bad king. They abolished the monarchy entirely and created something new: a republic where power was shared, limited, and temporary.

The word "republic" comes from *res publica,* meaning "the public thing" or "the people's affair." The idea was that Rome belonged to its citizens collectively, not to one man. This was radical for its time. Most ancient societies were monarchies or oligarchies. Rome tried something different. The ancient Romans created a system with built-in checks to prevent any individual from accumulating too much power.

Instead of one king, Rome would have two consuls who shared executive power and served for only one year. They could veto each other's decisions, which meant they had to cooperate, or nothing would get done. After their year in office, they returned to being ordinary citizens (though usually very prominent ones). This system prevented anyone from becoming a permanent ruler.

The Senate, which had existed under the kings as an advisory council, gained real power. Senators were former magistrates, usually wealthy landowners with military experience. They controlled foreign policy, public finances, and religious matters. While they could not pass laws on their own, their authority (called *auctoritas*) gave their opinions enormous weight.

The citizen assemblies voted on laws and elected magistrates. There were several different assemblies organized in different ways, and over time, the system became incredibly complicated. However, the basic idea was that Roman citizens had a direct voice in government.

This new system was not a democracy in the modern sense. Power remained concentrated among wealthy families. Poor citizens had less influence than rich ones. Women could not vote. Slaves had no rights at all. But compared to a monarchy, it was revolutionary. Power was distributed and limited. Legal protections developed gradually, most notably with the Twelve Tables around 450 BCE, which codified laws and made them publicly available so that judges could not simply invent rules as they pleased.

The early Roman Republic was chaotic. Tarquin tried multiple times to retake Rome by force, enlisting the help of other Etruscan cities and Lars Porsena, the king of Clusium. Roman legend is full of heroes from this period: Horatius Cocles defending a bridge single-handedly, Mucius Scaevola burning his own hand to show Roman determination, Cincinnatus leaving his plow to save Rome and then returning to his farm afterward. These stories were probably exaggerated, but they reflected real conflicts as Rome fought to preserve its independence.

Rome's survival depended on alliances with other Latin cities. The Latins were a group of related peoples who spoke similar languages, worshiped similar gods, and faced similar threats from the hill tribes around them. Around 493 BCE, Rome joined the Latin League, a defensive alliance of about thirty Latin cities. The treaty, called the Foedus Cassianum after the Roman consul Spurius Cassius who negotiated it, established mutual defense and trade rights. If one city was attacked, the others helped. It was a practical arrangement born of necessity.

But Rome was never content being just a member of the alliance. Over the next century, Rome gradually shifted from partner to leader to overlord. When Latin cities rebelled in 340 BCE during the Latin War, Rome crushed them and dissolved the Latin League. The rebel cities lost their independence. Some were incorporated directly into Rome. Others became Roman allies with obligations to provide troops but had no say in policy. This pattern of alliance, dominance, and absorption became Rome's standard operating procedure for the next several centuries.

The early Roman Republic also faced constant warfare closer to home. The Aequi and Volsci, tribal peoples from the central Italian hills, raided Roman territory almost annually. These were not grand campaigns, just bands of warriors stealing crops, burning farms, and driving off livestock. Rome had to defend itself every fighting season, which meant Roman men spent much of each year in arms. This constant low-level conflict turned Rome into a militarized society where every citizen was expected to serve in the army. Military success was seen as the path to political power.

The republic also faced internal tensions from the start. Two classes of citizens emerged: patricians (wealthy aristocratic families) and plebeians (everyone else). The patricians monopolized political power, holding all the important positions and controlling the Senate. The plebeians, who made up the bulk of the army and the population, had voting rights but limited actual power.

The Romans had replaced a system that concentrated power in one person with a system that distributed power among many. They had traded stability for liberty, certainty for competition. It was messy, inefficient, and prone to deadlock.

The hatred of kingship became foundational to Roman identity. The very word "king" (*rex*) became an insult. Romans tolerated dictators appointed for six-month emergencies and military strongmen who ruled everything but did not hold the title king, but they never accepted the idea of a permanent hereditary monarch. When Julius Caesar flirted with accepting a crown centuries later, it helped get him killed.

This anti-monarchical attitude created a paradox at the heart of the Roman government. Romans wanted strong leadership but feared giving anyone too much power. They needed quick decision-making, but they had to face delays and vetoes. They admired military success but worried about successful generals becoming tyrants. This tension never got resolved. Instead, it created a dynamic political culture where ambition and restraint constantly battled each other.

The Roman Republic's structure also made Rome surprisingly adaptable. When something did not work, Romans could adjust it without overthrowing the entire system. The plebeians could win new rights without destroying the patrician class. New magistracies could be created when needed. The rules were not written in stone; they evolved based on precedent, negotiation, and sometimes mob action. This flexibility let Rome survive crises that might have shattered more rigid systems.

It was also the foundation for everything Rome would become. The republic, with all its internal conflicts and constitutional complications, would last nearly five hundred years. It would conquer Italy, defeat Carthage, and build an empire that stretched from Spain to Syria. The governmental structures created in 509 BCE–the consuls, Senate, and assemblies–would survive even after the Roman Republic died and emperors took control.

But none of that was obvious in 509 BCE. Back then, Rome was just one Latin city among many, distinguished mainly by having recently kicked out its king and invented a new form of government that probably seemed overly complicated to its neighbors.

The mud huts were still there. The population was maybe thirty thousand to forty thousand people total, most of them farmers. Nobody could have predicted that this small city on seven hills would eventually rule the Mediterranean world.

But the Romans had one thing going for them: they were incredibly stubborn. They did not quit. When they lost battles, they raised new armies. When other cities tried to conquer them, they fought back and then conquered those cities instead. When their government did not work, they adjusted it without abandoning the basic structure.

Rome was not founded in a day, despite what Romulus supposedly claimed. It was built gradually, messily, and violently over the centuries. The mud huts eventually became marble temples. The swamp became the Forum Romanum, the center of a world empire. The farmers became the legions that no one could defeat.

But it all started here, in the early republic, when Rome was small, vulnerable, and just beginning to figure out what it wanted to be.

# Chapter 2: The Republic: Power to the People (Sort Of)

## SPQR Explained: What "The Senate and the People of Rome" Actually Meant

If you've ever seen a Roman eagle standard, a manhole cover in Rome, or a tattoo on someone who really loves ancient history, you've probably seen the letters "SPQR." It stands for *Senatus Populusque Romanus* ("the Senate and the People of Rome").

These four letters summed up the Roman political identity. Power belonged to both the elite ("the Senate") and the citizens ("the People"). It was stamped on official documents, carved into public buildings, and painted on military standards. It appeared on aqueducts, triumphal arches, and even sewer covers. SPQR was Rome's brand, and Romans used it everywhere, not just during the republic but throughout the imperial period as well. During the Roman Empire, emperors' names often appeared alongside SPQR on coins and monuments.

But what did it actually mean in practice?

The phrase suggested a partnership between two groups. "The Senate" represented Rome's aristocratic elite. They were experienced statesmen, former magistrates, and wealthy landowners who advised on policy and controlled public finances. "The People" (*Populus*) represented the citizen body, but this did not mean all residents of Rome. It meant free male citizens. These men voted in assemblies, served in the army, and theoretically held ultimate sovereignty. Women, slaves, freedmen, and foreign residents were not part of the *Populus*, even though they made up most of Rome's actual population.

Notice the word "theoretically." In reality, SPQR was more slogan than substance, at least in the early Roman Republic. The Senate held most of the real power. Senators were not elected; they were appointed by the censors (magistrates who conducted the census and managed public morals) based on prior service as magistrates. Once you became a senator, you usually served for life unless you did something spectacularly disgraceful. The Senate controlled foreign policy, managed state finances, assigned military commands, and directed Rome's religious activities. While the Senate could not technically pass laws or formally veto them (only the assemblies could legislate), the Senate's influence often prevented magistrates from advancing proposals it opposed. Through procedure, religious interpretation, and social pressure, senators could effectively kill legislation without casting a formal veto.

How did the Senate wield this kind of power without formal legal authority? They did so through a combination of prestige, wealth, and social networks. When a magistrate took office, he consulted the Senate before making major decisions. Ignoring senatorial advice was legal but politically suicidal. Senators controlled the patronage networks that determined political careers. They had the wealth to fund elections. They had the social connections to make or break reputations. A young politician who defied the Senate might find himself without support for future campaigns. He would be excluded from profitable governorships or socially ostracized.

Senate membership worked like this. Once you served as quaestor (the entry-level magistracy), you were typically enrolled in the Senate at the next census. The censors could refuse to enroll someone or expel existing senators for moral failings, but this was rare. Most former magistrates remained senators for life. This meant the Senate was a self-perpetuating body of experienced politicians who had proven themselves worthy of high office.

The Senate also controlled Rome's finances through its oversight of the treasury. Want to fund a military campaign? The Senate decided. Need money for public works? The Senate allocated it. Planning to distribute grain to the poor? The Senate had to approve the expenditure. This financial control gave senators enormous leverage over ambitious magistrates who needed resources to achieve their goals.

Senatorial debates followed established customs. The presiding magistrate, usually a consul, would pose a question to the Senate. Experienced senators typically dominated the debate, often speaking at length. Senior ex-consuls and ex-praetors commanded the most attention, while junior senators frequently found themselves waiting for opportunities to speak that might never come. When it came time to vote, senators physically moved to stand with whichever proposal they supported. There were no secret ballots; everyone could see where you stood, literally.

The *Populus*, meanwhile, had voting rights but limited practical power, especially early on. The assemblies could pass laws and elect magistrates, but they could not propose legislation on their own—only magistrates could do that. Tribunes, however, gained increasing legislative power over time, especially after the *Lex Hortensia* in 287 BCE declared that plebiscites (decisions of the plebeian assembly) bound all citizens, not just plebeians. This gave tribunes significant power to propose and pass legislation. Even so, if the Senate opposed something, it could usually find ways to obstruct it. The assemblies were also structured to give more weight to wealthy voters than to poor ones.

So, SPQR represented an ideal more than a reality. Rome claimed to balance aristocratic wisdom with popular sovereignty. The Senate provided expertise and stability. The People provided legitimacy and military manpower. Together, they supposedly governed Rome.

This tension between elite control and popular participation defined Roman politics for centuries. The patricians wanted to preserve their privileges. The plebeians wanted a greater share of power. The Senate wanted authority without accountability. The assemblies wanted influence without chaos. Nobody was entirely happy, which meant everyone had to negotiate, compromise, and occasionally threaten violence to get what they wanted.

Ironically, as plebeians won access to magistracies and entered the Senate, senatorial power actually increased. The expanded Senate became even more dominant in foreign policy and finances, creating an oligarchy that included both patrician and wealthy plebeian families—what historians call the *nobiles*, or nobility.

The fact that the Romans bothered to carve SPQR on everything shows they believed the concept mattered. They did not call themselves "the Senate of Rome" or "the Roman People." They insisted on both. The

Senate could not claim absolute authority without acknowledging the People. The People could not claim total sovereignty without respecting the Senate. The partnership might have been unequal and contested, but it was real enough that both sides had to maintain the fiction.

Over time, as plebeians gained more rights and political power, SPQR became slightly less fictional. However, even at the end of the republic, when populist politicians like Julius Caesar claimed to represent "the People" against "the Senate," both sides still invoked SPQR. It was Rome's political identity, the idea that legitimate government required both aristocratic leadership and popular consent, however you defined those terms.

### Patricians vs. Plebeians: The Original Class Struggle

When the Roman Republic began in 509 BCE, Roman society split into two distinct legal classes: patricians and plebeians. This was not about wealth, though patricians were generally richer. It was about birth, legal status, and access to political power.

The patricians were Rome's original aristocratic families. They were the descendants of the senators Romulus supposedly appointed. There were only about a dozen or so patrician clans (*gentes*) in early Rome, including families like the Cornelii, the Fabii, the Claudii, and the Aemilii. These families claimed they alone had the right to hold religious offices, serve as magistrates, and sit in the Senate. They had exclusive knowledge of the law (which was not written down yet) and exclusive access to the gods through special religious rituals. Patricians could not legally marry plebeians until 445 BCE.

Everyone else was a plebeian. This included poor farmers, urban workers, merchants, and even some quite wealthy families who simply were not patrician by birth. Plebeians could vote in assemblies and serve in the army, but they could not hold major political offices or know whether patrician judges were applying laws fairly.

This system was inherently unstable. The patricians needed plebeian soldiers to defend Rome and expand its territory. The plebeians needed patrician leadership and legal protection. But the patricians wanted to hoard political power, and the plebeians increasingly resented being treated as second-class citizens.

The social divide ran deeper than just legal status. Roman society operated on a system of patronage. Wealthy patricians served as *patroni* (patrons) to poorer citizens who became their *clientes* (clients). A patron provided legal protection, financial support, and political advocacy for his clients. In return, clients voted how their patron wanted, showed up to support him in public, and helped enhance his prestige. A wealthy senator might have hundreds of clients who voted as a bloc in assemblies.

This patron-client system reinforced patrician power. Even when plebeians gained voting rights, their votes were often controlled by patrician patrons. Poor citizens depended on wealthy patrons for survival. You could not easily vote against the man who loaned you money, represented you in court, or helped your son get a job. The system was not exactly coercive, but it created obligations that limited political independence.

The result was the Conflict of the Orders, a two-hundred-year struggle that shaped the Roman Republic more than any war or conquest. The conflict began around 494 BCE, just fifteen years after the republic was founded. According to tradition, plebeian soldiers got fed up with fighting wars for patrician commanders while getting no say in government. Many plebeian farmers had fallen into debt. They had been away fighting and could not work their land, so they borrowed money at high interest rates. When they could not repay, creditors could enslave them. Patrician magistrates and judges naturally sided with patrician creditors.

We should note that our sources for these early events, primarily the historian Livy, who wrote around five hundred years after the fact, used literary conventions and dramatic storytelling to reconstruct a period for which they had limited reliable information. We lack contemporary records from the early Roman Republic. The basic outline of a patrician-plebeian conflict is almost certainly real, but specific details like speeches and dramatic scenes follow narrative patterns common to ancient historiography rather than documented historical records.

The plebeians responded with what we would now call a general strike, though the Romans called it a *secessio*. Plebeian soldiers marched out of Rome to the Sacred Mount, a hill a few miles from the city, and refused to come back. They essentially said, "We're done fighting your wars and working your fields until you treat us fairly."

This was a brilliant tactic. Rome faced external threats from neighboring peoples. Without plebeian soldiers, the city was defenseless. The patricians had to negotiate.

The result was a compromise. The plebeians got their own representatives called tribunes of the plebs. Tribunes were sacrosanct, which means they were legally protected by religious law. Anyone who harmed a tribune could be killed on the spot. Tribunes had the power of *intercessio*; they could veto any magistrate's action or any Senate decision. However, this power had a crucial limitation. A tribune had to be personally present to say "veto" (Latin for "I forbid"). He could not leave Rome's city limits, and tradition required that his house door remain open at night so any citizen seeking help could reach him. The plebeians also gained their own assembly, the *Concilium Plebis*, where they could meet and discuss issues without patrician interference.

### How the Government Worked: Consuls, Senate, and Assemblies

The Roman government was deliberately complicated. The whole system was designed to prevent any individual from accumulating too much power while still allowing the state to function. It was inefficient and prone to gridlock, but it was also remarkably durable.

Let's start with the magistrates—the elected officials who ran the government.

At the top were the consuls. Two consuls served for one year. They commanded armies, presided over the Senate, enforced laws, and essentially served as heads of state. Each consul could veto the other, which forced them to cooperate or at least negotiate. After their year in office, former consuls usually joined the Senate and often received provincial governorships where they could recoup the money they'd spent on elections and gain military glory.

Below the consuls were praetors, who administered justice. Initially, there was one praetor, but as Rome expanded, more were added. By the late Roman Republic, there were eight praetors handling different courts and provinces. Praetors could also command armies if needed.

Aediles managed Rome's infrastructure, such as roads, public buildings, the water supply, and markets. They also organized public games, which were expensive but great for building popularity if you had political ambitions.

Quaestors handled finances. They managed the treasury, supervised tax collection, and served as financial officers for generals in the field. Serving as quaestor typically qualified a man for Senate membership, though this remained subject to censorial review during the census.

Censors were senior magistrates elected every five years. They conducted the census (counting citizens and assessing their property) and could expel senators for disgraceful behavior. This wasn't just informal social pressure. Censors held formal power called the *regimen morum* (regulation of morals). They could issue a *nota* (mark of ignominy) that stripped a man of his rank, expelled him from the Senate, or removed him from his voting tribe. Censors had enormous authority, though they served only eighteen months and faced political backlash if they wielded their power unfairly.

Tribunes of the plebs represented plebeian interests and could veto magistrates' actions and Senate decisions through their power of *intercessio.* There were ten tribunes, and they served for one year. Tribunes couldn't leave Rome during their term; their power depended on being physically available to intervene when needed.

All these magistracies followed the *cursus honorum* (the "course of honors"), a traditional sequence of offices. You started as quaestor (minimum age thirty), then aedile, then praetor (minimum age thirty-nine), and then consul (minimum age forty-two). You had to wait two years between offices, and you couldn't serve in the same office twice in a row, though this rule was often violated later. The system was supposed to ensure experienced, mature leadership and prevent anyone from dominating politics.

Then there was the Senate. Technically, the Senate was just an advisory body. It couldn't pass laws or command armies directly. However, in practice, it was the most powerful institution in Rome.

Senators were former magistrates. Once you served as quaestor or in a higher position, you entered the Senate for life (unless the censors kicked you out). There were about three hundred senators during most of the Roman Republic. They sat on benches in the Senate House or various temples, debating policy and issuing *senatus consulta*—advisory opinions that magistrates almost always followed.

The Senate controlled foreign policy, declared states of emergency, assigned military commands, and managed public finances. Senators had enormous prestige and informal authority. When the Senate "advised" a consul to take a certain action, that consul usually took it. Defying the Senate was politically dangerous, as you could make powerful enemies who could wreck your career.

Finally, there were the assemblies where citizens voted on laws and elected magistrates. Rome had several different assemblies organized in different ways.

The *Comitia Centuriata* (Centuriate Assembly) voted on declarations of war, elected consuls and praetors, and passed laws. It was organized by wealth. Citizens were divided into groups called centuries based on how much property they owned and what military equipment they could afford.

The *Comitia Tributa* (Tribal Assembly) elected lower magistrates and voted on laws. It was organized by tribes (geographic districts). This was more democratic than the Centuriate Assembly but still gave more weight to property-owning citizens.

The *Concilium Plebis* (Plebeian Council) was the plebeian-only assembly where tribunes were elected and plebiscites were passed. After 287 BCE, its laws became binding for the entire Roman population.

The voting process itself was time-consuming and chaotic. On voting days, citizens gathered at dawn. A magistrate would take the auspices. This means they would check for divine approval by watching birds or examining animal entrails. If the omens were bad, voting was postponed. If the omens were good, voting proceeded. This system could be manipulated strategically. A magistrate opposed to a particular vote could announce he had observed unfavorable omens (*obnuntiatio*), effectively dissolving the assembly before it could vote.

Voting in Roman assemblies wasn't like modern elections. Citizens didn't cast individual ballots that were counted separately. Instead, each century or tribe voted internally and then cast one collective vote. Assemblies met in the Forum or on the Campus Martius, and voting was public. You walked to one side or another to indicate your choice. This made it easy for wealthy patrons to monitor how their clients voted.

The Centuriate Assembly's structure particularly favored the wealthy. Citizens were divided into 193 centuries based on property classes, though the exact numbers and organization varied over time, and our reconstruction relies on later sources. The wealthiest class (those who could afford full cavalry equipment) controlled eighteen centuries. The next wealthiest class (heavy infantry) controlled eighty centuries. Together, these two groups had ninety-eight centuries—a majority. This meant that if the wealthy classes agreed on something, voting stopped before the poorer classes even got to vote. The poorest citizens, grouped into just one century out of 193, almost never had any influence on the outcome.

This system had obvious flaws. Wealthy citizens had disproportionate influence. Voting was public, making intimidation possible. The presiding magistrate controlled the process and could manipulate procedures. Religious officials could declare bad omens to stop votes they didn't like. And since only citizens in Rome could vote (there was no absentee ballot system), farmers from distant regions often couldn't participate because traveling to Rome meant abandoning their farms during the planting or harvest seasons.

The whole system was designed with checks and balances. No individual could dominate the system for long. Power was distributed among multiple institutions with overlapping authorities. Ambitious politicians had to build coalitions, make deals, and compromise.

The downside was that the system worked best when everyone agreed to play by the unwritten rules. When politicians started breaking norms by extending their terms, using violence, or ignoring vetoes, the whole structure became unstable. By the late republic, ambitious generals with loyal armies were able to bypass the traditional system entirely, which is how the Roman Republic eventually died.

But for centuries, this complicated mess of magistrates, senators, and assemblies actually worked. It allowed Rome to conquer Italy, defeat Carthage, and build an empire.

### The Citizen-Soldier: Why the Roman Farmer Was the Most Dangerous Man in the Mediterranean

Rome's greatest strength wasn't its government or its laws. It was its soldiers.

Other ancient states had professional armies or hired mercenaries. Rome relied on citizen-soldiers—farmers who fought for part of the year, then returned home to plant crops. This system turned out to be Rome's secret weapon.

Every Roman citizen was liable for military service. By the late Roman Republic, men typically served from age seventeen to their mid-forties. When Rome needed an army, the consuls held a levy. Citizens gathered on Capitoline Hill, and tribunes selected men based on property qualifications and physical fitness. Richer citizens served in the cavalry. Middling property owners formed the heavy infantry. Poorer citizens served as light infantry or support troops. The very poorest, called *proletarii* (those who contributed only children, not property), were usually exempt from the heavy infantry but could be called to serve as rowers in the navy or as auxiliaries during emergencies.

Once selected, soldiers served for a campaign season, usually from spring through fall. During winter, the legions disbanded, and the soldiers went home. If Rome needed them again the following year, they were recalled. A citizen might serve six or seven campaigns over his lifetime, sometimes more during major wars.

Soldiers weren't paid much initially; they received a small stipend and whatever loot they captured. They had to provide their own weapons and armor, which was why military service was tied to property ownership. A heavy infantryman needed a helmet, body armor, a shield, a spear, and a sword. This wasn't cheap.

Nevertheless, the system worked brilliantly for several reasons.

First, citizen-soldiers fought for their own land, families, and city. Mercenaries fought for pay and went home when the money ran out. Roman citizens fought because losing meant their farms could be burned and their families could be enslaved. This gave them motivation that no amount of money could buy.

The connection between land ownership and military service created a vested interest in victory. When Rome conquered new territory, that land could be distributed to citizens who had served in the conquering army, though such distributions were often contested and politically charged. The Gracchi brothers' land reform efforts in the 2nd century BCE would demonstrate just how explosive this issue could become. Still, the possibility that military service might lead to land ownership meant that even poor citizens had economic incentives to support Rome's conquests. Veterans of successful campaigns might receive a small plot of land, turning them into property-owning citizens with even more reason to defend Rome's interests.

Second, Rome could raise new armies incredibly quickly. Other states had limited military manpower. If their professional army were destroyed, they were done. Rome could lose an entire legion and raise another within weeks. As long as Rome had citizens who met the property qualification, it had soldiers. This meant Rome could absorb defeats that would have crushed other states. During the Second Punic War, Rome lost multiple armies to Hannibal–something like fifty thousand to eighty thousand men in just a few battles–yet kept fighting because it could replace those losses.

Rome's Italian allies amplified this advantage. By the 3rd century BCE, Rome had bound most of Italy into a network of alliances. Allied cities had to provide troops when Rome demanded them. These allied contingents, called *socii,* often equaled or outnumbered Roman legionaries in any given army. This effectively doubled or tripled Rome's available manpower. When Rome fielded an army of forty thousand men, roughly half were Roman citizens, and half were Italian allies. If that army got destroyed, Rome could raise another Roman legion and demand more allied troops.

Third, the system distributed military experience throughout the population. Many Roman citizens had combat experience. They understood tactics, discipline, and how armies worked. This created a militarized society where military values—courage, discipline, and endurance—were deeply respected. It also meant Rome had a large pool of veterans who could be recalled in emergencies.

Fourth, citizen-soldiers had a stake in Roman politics. Since they risked their lives for Rome, they demanded political rights in return. This was what drove the Conflict of the Orders; plebeians who fought expected political power. The connection between military service and citizenship became fundamental to the Roman identity.

The basic military unit was the legion. By the middle of the Roman Republic, a legion had about 4,200 infantry and 300 cavalry. It was organized into smaller units called maniples, which consisted of about 120 men each. Maniples could move independently, which gave the legion flexibility. Roman soldiers fought in a checkerboard formation. Maniples in the front line covered gaps in the second line, which covered gaps in the third line. This meant Romans could rotate fresh troops into combat while tired ones fell back, maintaining pressure on their enemies. The earlier legion structure was likely less standardized.

It's worth noting that many of our detailed descriptions of Roman training methods come from Vegetius, a military writer from the late 4th century CE—hundreds of years after the Roman Republic fell. While these practices likely had earlier origins, we should be cautious about assuming all soldiers of the Roman Republic trained exactly as later sources describe. That said, the core emphasis on discipline, formation fighting, and practical weapons drill certainly characterized Roman military culture throughout their history.

Roman soldiers were famously disciplined. They trained constantly in weapons drill and formation fighting. They could march twenty miles a day carrying sixty to eighty pounds of gear. They built fortified camps every night when on campaign, even if they only planned to stay one night.

The nightly camp construction was particularly impressive. When a Roman army stopped for the evening, every soldier knew exactly what to do. The army would halt in formation. Scouts would reconnoiter the area and mark out the camp's boundaries. Then, while cavalry and light troops provided security, the heavy infantry would dig a defensive ditch around the entire perimeter, usually about three feet deep and three feet wide. The dirt from the ditch would form a rampart behind it. Sharpened stakes carried by soldiers would be planted on top of the rampart, creating a palisade. Inside, the camp would be laid out in a standardized grid pattern. The commander's tent would be in the center, legion quarters would be in specific blocks, and storage areas would be in designated spots. Every camp looked the same, so soldiers always knew where everything was.

This process took about three hours and required every soldier to work. The result was a fortified position that could withstand attacks and provide security for sleeping troops. Roman armies could march deep into enemy territory and sleep safely every night because they built these fortifications. When the army moved out the next morning, they'd sometimes burn the camp, although they sometimes left it standing; it depended on whether they planned to return.

Recruits practiced with wooden swords heavier than actual weapons, building strength and muscle memory. They trained against wooden posts, learning to thrust rather than slash. The *gladius* was designed for stabbing. It was shorter than most swords, about eighteen to twenty-four inches, with a sharp point. Roman training emphasized repeated thrusting motions at vital points, primarily the throat, abdomen, and groin. Slashing exposes your body to a counterattack. Thrusting from behind a shield is safer and more lethal.

Roman tactics emphasized close combat. The heavy infantry carried a rectangular shield (*scutum*), a short sword (*gladius*), and two javelins (*pila*). They'd throw the javelins at close range to disrupt enemy formations and then charge in with swords.

Roman soldiers also built things. They constructed roads, bridges, siege equipment, and fortifications. Every legionary was part engineer. This made Roman armies incredibly versatile. They could besiege cities, storm fortifications, build supply lines, and fight pitched battles.

The citizen-soldier system did have limits, though. Constant warfare hurt Roman farmers. If you spent months away on campaign every year, your farm suffered. Your family struggled. You fell into debt. By the 2$^{nd}$

century BCE, many small farmers couldn't afford to keep serving. They would lose their land to debt and no longer meet the property qualification.

The problem got worse as Rome's wars moved farther from home. In the early Roman Republic, campaigns were seasonal and local. Romans fought nearby Latin cities, Etruscan towns, or hill tribes. One could march out in spring, fight through summer, and be home by fall harvest. But as Rome expanded into southern Italy, then Sicily, then Spain and Greece, campaigns lasted longer and took soldiers farther from their farms. A campaign in Spain might keep you away for three or four years. Your farm couldn't survive that.

Meanwhile, wealthy landowners prospered. They bought failing farms from indebted soldiers. They used slave labor captured in Rome's wars to work their expanding estates. Large slave-run farms, called *latifundia*, produced more efficiently than small family farms. This created a vicious cycle: wars produced slaves who displaced small farmers, who fell into debt and lost their land, which made them ineligible for military service, which threatened Rome's ability to fight more wars.

For centuries, though, the citizen-soldier system made Rome nearly invincible. Rome could lose battles and bounce back. It could fight multiple wars simultaneously on different fronts. It could grind down opponents through sheer persistence. Hannibal killed over fifty thousand Romans at Cannae in 216 BCE—the worst military defeat in Roman history—yet Rome refused to surrender and eventually won the war.

By the time the Roman Republic entered its imperial phase in the 2nd century BCE, Rome had created one of the most effective military systems the ancient Mediterranean had ever seen. It wasn't the biggest army, as other states could field larger forces. It also wasn't the most sophisticated; Greek armies had better tactical theory. What made Rome unstoppable wasn't size or sophistication. It was endurance, adaptability, and a knack for turning allies into assets. No rival could match that combination.

Rome won wars not because it won every battle but because it never stopped fighting. It could replace losses that would have ended other states, and it bound allies and conquered peoples into its system. Its citizens believed Rome was worth dying for and that military service made them part of something greater than themselves. They were the Senate and People of Rome, carved into monuments and carried on standards. They were SPQR, and they conquered most of the known world.

# Chapter 3: The Punic Wars: Rome Meets Its Match

## The Rise of Carthage: Rome's First "Superpower" Rival

By 264 BCE, Rome had dominated most of the Italian Peninsula through conquest and alliances. It had spent two centuries conquering its neighbors, absorbing them into alliances, and building a military system that seemed unstoppable. Roman legions had defeated the Samnites, the Etruscans, and even the Greek general Pyrrhus, whose victories were so costly that "Pyrrhic victory" entered the language as a term for winning at an unsustainable price.

Rome was powerful. But it wasn't the most powerful state in the Mediterranean. That distinction belonged to Carthage.

Carthage sat on the coast of North Africa in what's now Tunisia. It was perfectly positioned to control trade across the Mediterranean. Founded around 814 BCE by Phoenician colonists from the city of Tyre in modern Lebanon, Carthage had grown into a commercial empire. While Rome conquered through military force, Carthage dominated through trade, colonies, and naval power.

But Carthage wasn't just a merchant city. The Carthaginians controlled the extraordinarily fertile Bagradas Valley (the modern Medjerda River valley) in Tunisia, which produced massive grain surpluses and supported a substantial agricultural population. Carthaginian expertise in agriculture was so renowned that when Rome eventually conquered Carthage, the Senate ordered the translation of Mago's agricultural treatise into Latin—

one of the few Carthaginian texts Romans bothered to preserve. Carthage's wealth came from a combination of agricultural production, tribute from subject territories, and maritime trade.

The Carthaginian republic (yes, Carthage had a republican government too, with elected officials and a council) controlled ports throughout the western Mediterranean, including Sicily, Sardinia, Corsica, southern Spain, and the North African coast. Carthaginian ships transported grain, metals, wine, olive oil, and luxury goods between these trading posts. The city's military reflected its commercial focus. Carthage relied heavily on hired mercenaries rather than citizen-soldiers for most campaigns, paying professional troops from various ethnic groups to fight its wars. Carthage did maintain elite citizen infantry units, often identified by ancient sources as the "Sacred Band," though modern scholars debate its size, composition, and exact role. These units were generally reserved for defending Carthaginian territory directly and were only deployed in the field during major crises.

The Carthaginian navy was the real power. Carthage fielded hundreds of warships, namely quinqueremes. These were powerful vessels with multiple rowers per oar station rather than five separate decks. They would be crewed by experienced sailors who could outmaneuver most opponents. Roman sources claimed Carthage could field 350 warships at its peak, though this number may be exaggerated. Still, Carthaginian naval dominance in the western Mediterranean was real. They dominated naval power, which meant they dominated trade, which meant they controlled a lot of wealth.

By the 3rd century BCE, Carthage was richer than Rome, more sophisticated, and seemingly more powerful. Carthaginian culture blended Phoenician traditions with Greek influences and African elements. They worshiped gods like Baal Hammon and Tanit. Roman propaganda later accused them of child sacrifice, though modern historians debate whether this actually happened or was just part of Rome's usual tactic of making its enemies look barbaric.

Rome and Carthage had coexisted peacefully for centuries, bound by treaties that divided spheres of influence. Carthage controlled the seas and focused on North Africa, Spain, and the Mediterranean islands. Rome dominated Italy and minded its own business. Neither state threatened the other's core interests.

Then the Mamertines screwed everything up.

The Mamertines were Italian mercenaries who had seized control of Messana (modern Messina) on the northeastern tip of Sicily. When Syracuse, a Greek city-state in Sicily, attacked them, the Mamertines asked Rome for help. This put Rome in an awkward position. The Mamertines were essentially pirates who had stolen a city. Helping them violated Roman principles. But Syracuse was allied with Carthage, and letting Carthage gain control of Messana would give the Carthaginians a foothold just across the narrow strait from Italy; barely two miles of water separated them from Rome's territory.

After much debate, Rome decided to intervene. Roman forces crossed into Sicily in 264 BCE. Carthage responded by sending its own troops. Neither side intended to start a massive war. Both just wanted to protect their interests in Sicily.

They ended up fighting for twenty-three years.

The First Punic War (264–241 BCE) was primarily a naval conflict. Rome started with a serious disadvantage since it barely had a navy. The Romans were land fighters. They'd built a few warships for fighting pirates, but they had nothing comparable to Carthage's fleet. Roman crews initially lacked Carthaginian seamanship and experience with advanced naval tactics.

**What the Roman Republic and the Carthaginian Empire looked like at the beginning of the First Punic War.**[6]

The war began on land in Sicily, where Rome won initial victories against Carthaginian forces. Roman legions proved superior to

Carthaginian mercenaries in infantry combat. However, Carthage controlled the sea, allowing it to supply its forces in Sicily while harassing Roman supply lines. Rome realized it couldn't win the war without challenging Carthaginian naval dominance.

So, the Romans did what they always did when faced with a problem: they studied it, adapted, and persisted.

According to Roman tradition, they captured a beached Carthaginian warship, studied its design, and built a hundred copies in just sixty days. Ancient writers loved this story, but modern historians think it's more legend than fact. The truth was probably messier. Rome had access to expert shipbuilders through its southern Italian allies, especially the Greek cities, which had been building warships for centuries. Rather than copying one boat, Rome likely tapped into this know-how and existing shipyards.

What mattered was the urgency. Rome rushed to build a fleet and trained its crews on land, lining up benches like oars and drilling the timing until their rowers moved as one. They also introduced the *corvus* (Latin for "raven"), a boarding bridge with a spike on the end. In battle, they'd drop it onto an enemy ship to lock the vessels together, turning sea battles into infantry brawls. If they couldn't out-sail the Carthaginians, they'd out-fight them instead.

It worked. Rome won its first major naval battle at Mylae in 260 BCE using the corvus. They won another at Ecnomus in 256 BCE. Ancient historians describe it as involving over 300,000 men total, which would make it the largest naval battle in ancient history, though these figures are likely inflated by sources like Polybius, who tended to emphasize the scale of conflicts.

The corvus gave Rome initial advantages, but it had serious drawbacks. The device was top-heavy, making ships less stable, particularly in rough weather. After Rome lost multiple fleets to storms in 255 and 253 BCE, the corvus disappeared from Roman naval tactics. Rome had to learn actual seamanship rather than relying on a boarding-bridge gimmick.

Rome even attempted to invade North Africa directly, landing an army under the consul Marcus Atilius Regulus. The invasion initially succeeded but ultimately failed when Carthage hired a Spartan mercenary general named Xanthippus, who crushed the Roman force. Regulus was captured, and later Roman legends claimed he was tortured to death, though this story may be propaganda.

Carthage, meanwhile, struggled with the long conflict. Mercenary armies were expensive, and even Carthage's wealth had limits. The Carthaginian government faced internal political disputes about whether to continue the war. Their general in Sicily, Hamilcar Barca, fought brilliantly with limited resources but couldn't force a decisive victory.

Finally, in 241 BCE, Rome scraped together enough money to build one more fleet. This fleet caught the Carthaginian navy near the Aegates Islands and destroyed it. Without naval support, Carthaginian forces in Sicily couldn't be supplied. Carthage sued for peace.

The peace terms were harsh. Carthage had to abandon Sicily entirely, pay Rome 3,200 talents of silver over ten years (an enormous sum), and give up any claim to Sicily's Greek cities. Sicily became Rome's first overseas province. This territory was ruled directly by Rome rather than governed by allies.

Rome had won but barely. The victory cost hundreds of thousands of lives and pushed Rome's resources to their limits. But Carthage had lost, and losing meant humiliation, financial ruin, and the beginning of a hunger for revenge that would explode two decades later when Hamilcar Barca's son decided to finish what his father had started.

That son's name was Hannibal.

## Hannibal's Elephants: The Tactical Genius Who Almost Burned Rome to the Ground

Hannibal Barca was probably the most dangerous enemy Rome ever faced. Over a sixteen-year campaign, he invaded Italy and—according to ancient sources—cost Rome well over 100,000 lives. He came closer to destroying Rome than anyone else until the barbarian invasions five centuries later.

He did all this while outnumbered, operating in enemy territory, and never receiving adequate support from his home government. Modern military historians still study his tactics. Napoleon Bonaparte admired him, as did the Duke of Wellington. Hannibal's crossing of the Alps with elephants is legendary, but his real genius was tactical. He understood how to use terrain, psychology, and combined arms to defeat enemies who should have crushed him.

After the First Punic War, Carthage faced a mercenary revolt when it couldn't pay its soldiers. Hamilcar Barca brutally suppressed the revolt, then took his family to Spain, where Carthage still had colonies and silver mines. Hamilcar spent years rebuilding Carthaginian power in Spain, creating a new empire and a new army loyal to his family rather than to the Carthaginian government.

Hamilcar made his son Hannibal swear an oath to hate Rome forever. When Hamilcar died, Hannibal's brother-in-law, Hasdrubal, took command. When Hasdrubal was assassinated, the army elected twenty-six-year-old Hannibal as their general. He was young, brilliant, and absolutely committed to destroying Rome.

The trigger for the Second Punic War (218–201 BCE) was Saguntum, a Spanish city allied with Rome. When Hannibal besieged it in 219 BCE, Rome protested. Hannibal captured and destroyed the city anyway. Rome demanded that Carthage hand over Hannibal, but Carthage refused. War began.

Everyone expected Hannibal to invade Sicily or Sardinia. Instead, he marched overland from Spain to Italy through the Alps, leading to one of history's most daring military maneuvers.

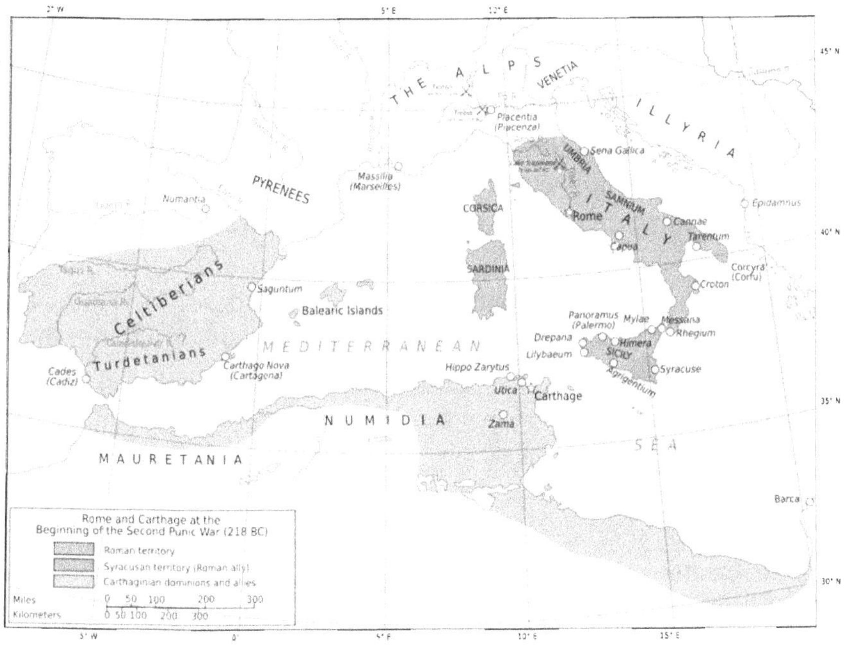


**The Roman Republic and Carthage at the beginning of the Second Punic War.**[7]

According to ancient estimates, Hannibal began with perhaps around fifty thousand infantry, several thousand cavalry, and a contingent of war elephants. The exact figures are debated, and they decreased significantly during the Alpine crossing. Scholars still argue about which specific Alpine pass Hannibal used. Several routes are possible, and ancient sources don't provide enough detail to be certain. What's clear is that the crossing was brutal. Snow, ice, rockslides, and attacks from hostile mountain tribes killed perhaps a third of his army. Most of the elephants died in the mountains or shortly afterward from the cold.

What made Hannibal's army remarkable wasn't its size but its composition and his ability to hold it together. His troops came from dozens of different peoples and included Iberians from Spain, Numidians from North Africa, Gauls from southern France and northern Italy, Libyans, Greeks, and various other mercenaries. They spoke different languages, worshiped different gods, and had different fighting styles. The Numidian cavalry were light horsemen, fast and mobile. The Spanish infantry were fierce close-combat fighters. The African infantry fought in disciplined formations influenced by Hellenistic tactics. Hannibal had to coordinate all these different groups, keep them supplied, maintain discipline, and prevent ethnic rivalries from tearing his army apart, all while operating in enemy territory with no reliable supply line to Carthage.

He managed it through a combination of personal charisma, shared hardship, and impressive tactical victories that kept his troops confident in his leadership. Hannibal shared the soldiers' hardships. He slept on the ground, wore the same basic gear as his troops, and was always visible during battles. He paid well when he could and distributed plunder fairly. Most importantly, he kept winning, and soldiers follow generals who deliver victories.

Hannibal made it. In autumn 218 BCE, he descended into the Po Valley in northern Italy with an army that, while smaller than what he'd started with, was hardened by the march and ready to fight.

Rome sent an army to stop him. Hannibal destroyed it at the Trebia River, using an ambush and his cavalry superiority to surround and annihilate the Roman force in the river valley.

Rome sent another army. Hannibal ambushed it at Lake Trasimene in 217 BCE, catching the Romans marching along a narrow path between the lake and the hills. Hannibal's troops attacked from the hills, driving the Romans into the lake. Some fifteen thousand Romans died, and the consul Gaius Flaminius was killed in the fighting. It was one of the largest ambushes recorded in ancient warfare.

Rome panicked. Two armies had been destroyed in two years. Hannibal was loose in Italy, and Rome couldn't stop him. The Senate appointed Quintus Fabius Maximus as dictator (an emergency position giving one man complete authority for six months). Fabius adopted a strategy of avoiding direct battle, shadowing Hannibal's army, and harassing his supply lines in the hopes of preventing him from capturing major cities. Romans mocked this cautious approach, calling Fabius "the Delayer." But it worked; it kept Rome from losing another army.

The Roman people, however, wanted victory, not delay. In 216 BCE, they elected two consuls–Gaius Terentius Varro and Lucius Aemilius Paullus–and gave them the largest army Rome had ever fielded: roughly eighty thousand infantry and six thousand cavalry. The Romans would crush Hannibal through sheer numbers.

The armies met at Cannae in southeastern Italy on August 2$^{nd}$, 216 BCE. What followed was the worst defeat in Roman military history and one of the most studied battles in military education.

Hannibal had about forty thousand infantry and ten thousand cavalry. He was outnumbered nearly two to one. He arranged his infantry in a crescent formation with his weaker Gallic and Spanish troops in the center and his elite African infantry on the flanks. His cavalry was on the wings.

The Romans attacked in their traditional dense formation, pushing forward to break Hannibal's center. The Carthaginian center gave ground, slowly retreating but staying intact. The Roman mass pushed deeper into the crescent, which gradually became a U-shape with Roman troops packed into the center.

Then Hannibal sprang the trap. His cavalry, which had defeated the Roman cavalry on both wings, swept around behind the Roman army. His African infantry on the flanks wheeled inward, attacking the Roman sides. The crescent had become an encirclement with the Romans trapped inside.

The Romans couldn't maneuver. They were packed too tightly, and as the encirclement tightened, the formation became increasingly ineffective. The soldiers in the middle couldn't effectively use their weapons; the press of bodies from all sides limited their ability to fight. Those in the rear kept pushing forward, not realizing they were forcing their comrades deeper into the killing zone. For hours, Carthaginian soldiers methodically attacked the compressed Roman formation from all sides.

By the end of the day, ancient sources report between fifty thousand and seventy thousand Roman deaths, though exact numbers are debated. The consul Paullus and the eighty senators who had volunteered to serve died. Hannibal's losses were around six thousand men.

According to the historian Livy, Hannibal's cavalry commander Maharbal urged him to march on Rome immediately, allegedly saying, "You know how to win a victory, Hannibal, but you don't know how to use one." Roman historians used dramatic quotes to create a more compelling narrative, so it is very possible these words were never uttered. Nevertheless, Hannibal didn't march on Rome. Modern historians debate why. Maybe Rome's walls were too strong, maybe his army was exhausted, maybe he lacked siege equipment, or maybe he believed Rome would negotiate. We just don't know.

What we do know is that this decision probably cost Carthage the war. Rome didn't surrender. Despite losing three major armies and over 100,000 men, despite several Italian allies defecting to Hannibal, despite Syracuse and Macedon allying with Carthage, Rome refused to negotiate.

Instead, Rome did what it always did. It raised more armies. It changed tactics. And it persisted.

Roman leaders refused to talk peace while Hannibal was still in Italy. They dealt harshly with cowards and deserters, often sending them into the toughest positions rather than letting them go free. To fill the ranks, Rome opened service to men who previously wouldn't have qualified and drew on wealthy citizens to finance the growing war effort.

Rome didn't try to beat Hannibal in a single big battle. Instead, it shadowed him and slowly chipped away at his support. When Hannibal threatened a town, Roman armies rushed in to defend it or cut off his supplies. When he left, they reclaimed territory and punished those who had sided with him. Rome's strategy was patient, and in the end, it wore Hannibal down.

Rome also strangled Hannibal's reinforcements. When his brother Hasdrubal finally crossed the Alps with a second Carthaginian army in 207 BCE, Rome intercepted him at the Metaurus River in northern Italy before he could link up with Hannibal. The Romans destroyed Hasdrubal's army and killed him. According to Livy, they catapulted his severed head into Hannibal's camp to let him know his brother was dead and no help was coming.

Hannibal spent years roaming Italy, winning tactical victories but unable to force a strategic victory. He couldn't capture Rome or any major Latin city. He couldn't break Rome's alliance system entirely. His supplies dwindled. Reinforcements from Carthage never came in sufficient numbers. The Carthaginian government was divided about supporting him, and Rome's navy controlled the sea lanes.

Rome, meanwhile, opened new fronts. They sent armies to Spain to cut off Carthaginian resources and reinforcements. They invaded North Africa to threaten Carthage itself. They slowly ground down Hannibal's strength through attrition.

Spain became the critical theater. Carthage's Spanish territories provided silver from mines, manpower from Iberian tribes, and a staging ground for reinforcements to Italy. The Barcid family—Hannibal's family—had built their power base there. Hannibal's father, Hamilcar, had conquered much of Spain. His brother-in-law, Hasdrubal the Fair, had founded New Carthage (Cartagena) as a major port and administrative center. When Hannibal left for Italy, he left his younger brother, Hasdrubal Barca, in command of Spain, with orders to hold it and send reinforcements.

Rome sent armies to contest Spain starting in 218 BC. The war there was vicious, with neither side able to gain a decisive advantage initially. In 211 BCE, disaster struck. Both Roman commanders in Spain, Publius Cornelius Scipio and his brother Gnaeus, were killed when their armies were separated and destroyed by superior Carthaginian forces.

This was when the Senate gave command to young Publius Cornelius Scipio. He was only twenty-five; he was technically too young for such a command under Roman law, but desperate times called for flexibility. Scipio knew that Spain wasn't just a sideshow. It was Hannibal's supply line and revenue source. Cut Spain away from Carthage, and Hannibal would wither in Italy.

The war lasted fifteen more years after Cannae. Hannibal remained undefeated in Italy; he was simply too skilled a commander. However, Rome had learned not to fight him on his terms.

### Scipio Africanus: The Man Who Learned Hannibal's Tricks and Used Them Against Him

Scipio had learned a hard lesson: Rome couldn't beat Hannibal by doing what Rome had always done. They needed to beat him at his own game.

Scipio didn't act like a typical Roman general. He was young, bold, and willing to break tradition. He trained his troops in new formations and drilled them until they could move quickly and fight as a unit. He studied cavalry tactics—something many Roman commanders ignored—and learned from Hannibal's greatest strength: combining different kinds of troops into one coordinated attack. Infantry, cavalry, speed, and surprise all had to work together. Scipio wasn't just copying Hannibal. He was adapting and getting ready to turn the tables.

In Spain, Scipio captured New Carthage (Cartagena) in a brilliant assault in 209 BCE, seizing Carthage's main Spanish base and cutting off Hannibal's supplies. He defeated multiple Carthaginian armies, driving them out of Spain entirely. He treated captured Spanish tribes honorably, turning many of them against Carthage. By 206 BCE, Rome controlled Spain.

Scipio returned to Rome a hero and pitched a bold plan: take the war to North Africa and force Carthage to call Hannibal back home. The Senate wasn't convinced. Most Romans wanted to get Hannibal out of Italy first. But Scipio had momentum. He was elected consul in 205 BCE and granted special command for the African invasion.

He didn't get much support from the government. But he built and trained his army in Sicily anyway. He drilled them in the fast, flexible tactics he'd studied from Hannibal, especially cavalry maneuvers and coordinated attacks that could break the stiff formations Rome usually relied on.

In 204 BCE, Scipio landed in North Africa with about thirty thousand men. Carthage was caught off guard. For over a decade, the war had been fought in Italy and Spain; now, suddenly, Rome was on their doorstep. Carthage formed an alliance with the Numidian king Syphax, who provided cavalry. Scipio allied with a rival Numidian prince named Masinissa, who brought his own cavalry to the Roman side.

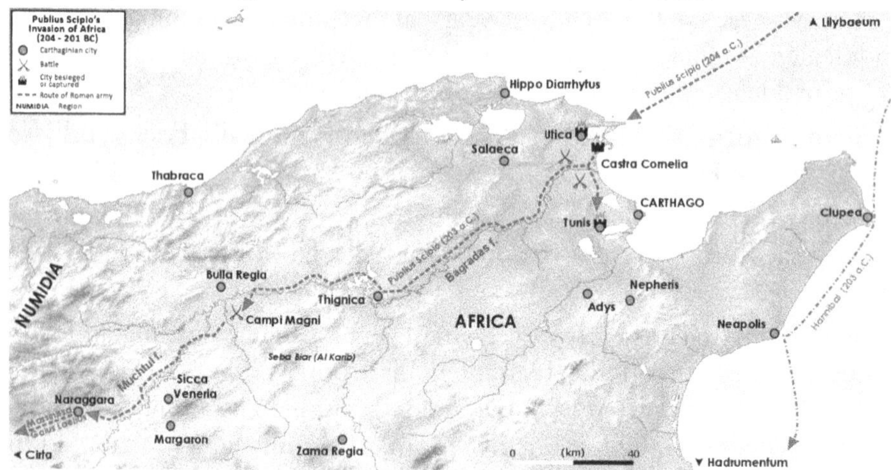


Scipio's campaign in North Africa.[8]

Scipio defeated the Carthaginian-Numidian coalition in several battles. He captured Syphax, besieged Carthaginian cities, and ravaged the countryside. Carthage panicked and recalled Hannibal Barca from Italy after fifteen years.

Hannibal returned to Africa having never lost a major battle in Italy. He still believed he could defeat Rome. But now he would face Scipio—the one Roman general who truly understood him.

The final confrontation came at the Battle of Zama in 202 BCE. The battle pitted two brilliant commanders against each other, both at the peak of their abilities.

According to ancient historians such as Polybius, Hannibal may have had around thirty-six thousand infantry, some cavalry, and a contingent of elephants. Scipio's forces numbered roughly twenty-nine thousand infantry and allied cavalry, primarily Numidian horsemen under Masinissa.

Hannibal planned to use his elephants to break up the Roman formation and then crush them with his veteran infantry from the Italian campaign. Scipio countered by arranging his infantry in columns with gaps between them. When the elephants charged, Roman trumpets and horns frightened many of them. Those elephants that did reach the Roman lines were channeled through the gaps Scipio had created, where skirmishers could attack them from the sides or simply let them pass through harmlessly. The elephant charge, which should have been devastating, achieved little.

The infantry lines clashed. Hannibal's front line of raw recruits gave ground against the disciplined Romans. His second line of Carthaginian citizen-soldiers fought harder but eventually broke. Hannibal kept his third line—his veterans from Italy—in reserve.

Meanwhile, Scipio's cavalry under Masinissa drove off Hannibal's cavalry, just as Hannibal's cavalry had done to the Romans at Cannae. The difference was that Scipio's cavalry returned to the battlefield and attacked Hannibal's veterans from behind.

Scipio had used Hannibal's own tactics against him. The Carthaginian army was surrounded and destroyed. Hannibal himself escaped with a small group of horsemen.

Carthage sued for peace. The terms were devastating. Carthage had to give up Spain and all the Mediterranean islands, surrender its entire navy except ten ships, pay an indemnity that ancient sources report as around ten thousand talents of silver over decades—an enormous sum that would cripple its economy—promise not to wage war outside Africa without Roman permission, and essentially become a Roman client state.

Hannibal advised the Carthaginian Senate to accept the terms. "We fought for empire," he reportedly said, "and we lost. Now we must accept the consequences." Carthage accepted.

Rome had won. Carthage would never again threaten Roman power. Scipio earned the cognomen *Africanus* for his victory and became one of Rome's greatest heroes.

Hannibal remained in Carthage for several years, reforming its government and finances. But his enemies in Carthage accused him of planning a new war with Rome. In 195 BCE, Rome demanded his extradition. Hannibal fled, spending the rest of his life wandering the eastern Mediterranean as a military advisor to various kings. He died around 183 BCE, allegedly by poison to avoid Roman capture. He was around sixty-five years old.

Roman historians claimed he spent his final years bitter and defeated. Or perhaps he simply realized what he'd always known: Rome would never stop, never surrender, and never accept anything less than total victory. He'd come closer to destroying Rome than anyone else would for centuries.

But close wasn't enough.

### "Carthage Must Be Destroyed": The Total Annihilation of a Rival

The Second Punic War ended in 201 BCE, but the story of Carthage and Rome wasn't finished. Fifty years of uneasy peace followed, during which Carthage recovered economically. The Carthaginians went back to what they did best: trade. Ancient sources suggest Carthage might have paid off its war indemnity ahead of schedule. The city prospered. By the mid-2nd century BCE, Carthage was once again wealthy, though it was no longer militarily powerful.

During this period, Rome was transforming. The victory over Carthage had made Rome the dominant power in the western Mediterranean. Rome turned its attention eastward, conquering Macedon and Greece, defeating the Seleucid Empire in Asia Minor, and establishing itself as the mediator of Mediterranean politics. Roman wealth increased enormously as tribute, slaves, and trade goods flowed into Italy. However, this wealth was unevenly distributed. It enriched senators and military commanders, while many small farmers who'd fought in the wars lost their land to debt.

Carthage, stripped of its empire and military, focused on agriculture and trade in North Africa. Markets flourished. The population grew. Carthaginian farmers cultivated the fertile lands around the city. Carthaginian merchants traded throughout Africa and the Mediterranean, though now as junior partners to Greek and Italian traders rather than as the dominant commercial power.

This prosperity bothered some Romans. One senator in particular, Marcus Porcius Cato, better known as Cato the Elder, became obsessed with the idea that Carthage posed a threat to Rome.

Cato had served in the Second Punic War. He'd seen what Hannibal could do. He believed that as long as Carthage existed, Rome faced danger. Cato allegedly ended every speech in the Senate, regardless of the topic, with the phrase *Carthago delenda est* ("Carthage must be destroyed").

Ancient sources report that Cato once brought fresh figs from Carthage to the Senate and pointed out how close Carthage was to Rome—just three days by sea—and how fertile and prosperous its territories remained. The implication was clear: Carthage could recover its military power if given time and opportunity.

Other senators thought Cato was paranoid. Carthage had no significant military and couldn't even wage war without Roman permission. It posed no threat. The real danger, they argued, was that Carthage's destruction would remove the external threat that kept Rome unified. As long as Carthage existed, the Romans had a common enemy. Without that enemy, Roman factions might turn on each other.

Both sides were right, though the second group was more right than they knew. Carthage wasn't a military threat, and destroying it would contribute to Rome's internal political collapse.

Rome destroyed Carthage anyway. The push for war came from a coalition of Roman interests. Some senators genuinely feared Carthage. Others saw war as an opportunity for military glory and political advancement. Some were connected to Italian merchants who wanted to eliminate Carthaginian commercial competition. And some Romans simply believed that a great power couldn't leave a former rival alive, even if that rival was now harmless.

Masinissa, Rome's Numidian ally who had helped defeat Hannibal, kept seizing Carthaginian territory. Masinissa was clever. He would provoke border incidents and then appeal to Rome to mediate. Rome consistently ruled in his favor. Over the decades, Carthage lost significant territory because of these seizures. When Carthage complained, Rome told them to accept the decisions. When Carthage tried to defend its borders militarily, Rome accused it of violating the treaty.

Finally, around 151 BCE, Carthage raised an army and attacked Masinissa without Roman permission, technically violating the peace treaty. The attack failed anyway, but Rome now had its excuse.

According to ancient accounts, Rome made increasingly harsh demands that pushed Carthage toward war. First, Rome demanded that Carthage hand over three hundred noble hostages. Carthage complied, desperate to avoid war. Then Rome demanded that Carthage surrender all weapons and armor. Carthage complied, sending thousands of sets of armor and catapults to the Roman army camped outside the city.

Then Rome revealed its final demand. The people had to abandon Carthage entirely, move at least ten miles inland, and build a new city away from the coast.

This was impossible. Carthage's wealth came from maritime trade. Moving inland meant economic death. The Carthaginians realized they'd been set up. Rome wanted war regardless of what Carthage did. The Romans intended to destroy them.

Carthage chose to fight. With no weapons or armor, the Carthaginians improvised. Women cut their hair to make bowstrings. Citizens melted down metal objects to make weapons.

The Third Punic War (149–146 BCE) was a siege, not a campaign. Rome sent an army under the consul Manius Manilius, but the initial Roman efforts were poorly executed. The Romans couldn't break through Carthage's walls or blockade the harbor effectively. The siege dragged on for three years with little progress.

In 147 BCE, Rome sent Scipio Aemilianus, the adopted grandson of Scipio Africanus, to take command. Scipio Aemilianus was a capable general who had served in Spain. He tightened the siege and built a mole (a large, manmade barrier) to block the harbor and starve the city.

By spring 146 BCE, Carthage was out of food. Scipio Aemilianus ordered the final assault. Roman troops breached the walls and fought street by street, house by house. The Carthaginians fought desperately, but they were starving and outnumbered. The battle lasted six days. Roman soldiers set fire to buildings with defenders still inside.

The last Carthaginians retreated to the Temple of Eshmun on Byrsa Hill. Some surrendered. Others, including the wife of the Carthaginian commander Hasdrubal (not the same Hasdrubal who was Hannibal's brother-in-law), threw themselves into the flames rather than surrender. Hasdrubal surrendered to Scipio, reportedly begging for mercy, which Roman sources used to mock him as a coward.

When the fighting ended, Scipio Aemilianus supposedly stood looking at the burning city and wept. According to Polybius, who was present, Scipio quoted Homer. "A day will come when sacred Troy shall perish, and Priam and his people shall be slain." When Polybius asked why he wept, Scipio said he was thinking of Rome and how all empires eventually fall.

Whether this story is true or a later invention is debated. What's certain is that Rome showed no mercy. Ancient sources report that tens of thousands of survivors were sold into slavery. Buildings were torn down. The harbor was destroyed. The site was later reoccupied, so claims that Romans plowed the ground and sowed it with salt to prevent anything from growing are false; this dramatic detail first appeared in 19th-century histories and has no ancient evidence to support it.

The destruction of Carthage was total. A civilization that had existed for nearly seven hundred years, that had controlled Mediterranean trade, that had produced Hannibal and challenged Rome's supremacy, ceased to exist. Only ruins remained.

The Punic Wars were over. Rome had survived Hannibal's invasion through stubborn persistence, adapted its tactics, and ultimately crushed its greatest rival. The victory made Rome master of the western Mediterranean and opened the path to further conquests in Greece, Asia Minor, and beyond.

# Chapter 4: The Crack in the Foundation

## The Cost of Victory: How Wealth and Slavery Destroyed the Roman Middle Class

Rome won the Punic Wars. It defeated Carthage, conquered Spain, and became the dominant power in the western Mediterranean. Victory brought staggering wealth, as gold, silver, slaves, and tribute poured into Italy. The 2nd century BCE should have been Rome's golden age.

Instead, victory nearly destroyed the Roman Republic.

Here was the problem. Rome got rich, but only some Romans got rich. The wars that made Rome powerful hollowed out the very foundation that had made Rome strong: the farmers who served as citizen-soldiers.

Think about how the system worked. Roman soldiers were citizens who owned property. They were mostly small farmers with five to twenty acres. They grew grain and raised some animals. When Rome needed soldiers, they left their farms to fight. A few months later, they came home, planted crops, and returned to civilian life.

This worked well when wars were short and close to home. Leave in spring, fight through summer, and be back for the fall harvest. Your family could manage while you were gone. But Rome's wars started to change. Campaigns in Spain lasted years. Wars in Greece and Asia Minor kept soldiers away for season after season. The Second Punic War dragged on for nearly two decades.

Long military service destroyed small farmers. Picture it. You're fighting in Spain for three years. Back home, your farm sits unworked. Your wife and children try to keep it going, but plowing and harvesting require a lot of strength. Production drops. The family falls into debt, borrowing money at brutal interest rates just to buy food and seed. When you finally get home—if you get home—you're facing debts you can't possibly repay.

Creditors foreclose. You lose your land. And without land, you can't serve in the army anymore. Rome just lost a soldier. This cycle repeated thousands of times across Italy.

Meanwhile, wealthy Romans were making a killing. Senators and wealthy businessmen (the equestrian class—essentially the business elite just below senators) bought up foreclosed farms. They consolidated small plots into massive estates called *latifundia*. These estates didn't grow grain for local markets. They produced cash crops, such as wine, olive oil, and wool, for export. And they didn't use free labor. They used slaves.

The same wars that destroyed small farmers produced an enormous supply of slaves. When Rome conquered a city, it often enslaved the entire population. By the late 2nd century BCE, Italy's slave population had exploded.

Slaves made economic sense for big landowners. Pay once up front, and then you only have to pay maintenance costs. They didn't have to pay slaves any wages. Slaves couldn't quit. They also couldn't join the army and abandon their work. Large estates using slave labor could produce more efficiently and focus on high-value exports. Rich landowners had money to invest in irrigation, storage, and processing equipment. They had political connections to secure favorable trade arrangements. Small farmers had no chance of competing.

By the 130s BCE, Roman officials conducting the census noticed the problem. The number of citizens who met the property qualification for military service was declining. Fewer citizens owned land. More landless poor crowded into Rome. The wealth gap between the rich and the poor was widening dramatically.

Some senators worried about military manpower. Others worried about social stability. A large population of poor, unemployed citizens was politically dangerous. They could be mobilized by ambitious politicians. They could riot. They needed food subsidies to survive, which strained public finances.

But most wealthy Romans weren't particularly concerned. They were profiting enormously from the existing system. Their estates were productive, and conquered provinces provided new investment opportunities. Why change a system that enriched the people who ran it?

Then, two brothers decided to fix the problem. They came from one of Rome's most prestigious families. Their names were Tiberius and Gaius Gracchus, and their reform efforts would trigger a century of political violence that would eventually destroy the Roman Republic they were trying to save.

## The Gracchi Brothers: The First True Populists

Tiberius Sempronius Gracchus was elected tribune of the plebs in 133 BC at the age of thirty. He came from the highest levels of Roman society. His father had been consul twice, and his mother was the daughter of Scipio Africanus, the hero who had defeated Hannibal. Ancient sources describe Tiberius's military service in Spain and Africa favorably. He had every reason to be a defender of the status quo.

Instead, he became a revolutionary.

Tiberius had seen the problem firsthand while traveling through Italy. He'd observed abandoned small farms, huge slave-run estates, and the decline of free citizens working the land. According to ancient sources, he was moved by the plight of displaced farmers and concerned about Rome's military capacity.

As tribune, Tiberius proposed land reform. The proposal was technically simple: enforce an old law that limited how much public land any individual could hold. Rome owned vast territories of *ager publicus* (Latin for "public land"), land conquered from enemies that theoretically belonged to the Roman state. In practice, wealthy Romans had occupied this public land and treated it as their own property, holding far more than the legal limit.

Tiberius's law would reclaim public land held beyond the legal limit and redistribute it to landless citizens in small plots. This would recreate the class of small farmers that Rome's military system required. Citizens would get land. Rome would gain soldiers. The Roman Republic would be saved.

The Senate opposed this. Most senators owned vast tracts of public land or had political connections to those who did. They didn't want to give up land they considered effectively theirs, even if it technically belonged to the state. They argued that Tiberius's proposal violated property rights and set a dangerous precedent by using popular politics to attack the wealthy.

Tiberius responded by taking his proposal directly to the people. He bypassed the Senate and brought his law before the Plebeian Assembly. This was technically legal, as tribunes could propose legislation to the assembly, but it violated an unwritten norm. Traditionally, important legislation was debated in the Senate first, and senators' views were respected even if they were not binding.

Tiberius broke that norm. He appealed to the urban poor and dispossessed farmers, arguing that the Senate was blocking reforms that would help ordinary citizens. Another tribune, Marcus Octavius, tried to veto Tiberius's law. According to ancient accounts, Tiberius responded by having the assembly vote to remove Octavius from office, a move that challenged traditional norms. Tribunes were sacrosanct (legally protected by religious law). Removing one was shocking.

But it worked. The law was passed. A commission was established to survey public lands and redistribute them. Tiberius, his brother Gaius, and his father-in-law, Appius Claudius Pulcher, would manage the process.

The Senate was furious but couldn't legally stop him. But then Tiberius made a fatal mistake: he announced he would run for tribune again. The tribunate was a one-year office. Running for immediate reelection was technically illegal and definitely a violation of tradition. Tiberius argued that his work wasn't finished and that his enemies would prosecute or kill him once he left office.

He was right about the second part.

On election day in 133 BCE, a group of senators and their supporters, led by the pontifex maximus (the highest religious office), Scipio Nasica (a cousin of Tiberius), formed a mob and attacked Tiberius and his followers. They beat Tiberius to death with clubs and wooden benches. Ancient sources report that about three hundred of his supporters were killed. The bodies were thrown into the Tiber River rather than receiving a proper burial.

This was unprecedented. Roman politics had been fierce before. There were insults, threats, and occasional scuffles. But murdering a tribune was something else entirely. By law and religion, tribunes were supposed to be untouchable. Harming one wasn't just illegal; it was sacrilege. Political violence had gone from angry words to outright murder, and the rules that kept Rome's system together suddenly felt breakable.

The Senate justified the murder by claiming Tiberius was trying to make himself king. The accusation was absurd. Tiberius was proposing land redistribution, not claiming royal power, but it served its purpose. Scipio Nasica and his accomplices faced no prosecution. The land commission continued its work, but without Tiberius's driving force, it eventually stalled and was disbanded.

Tiberius's younger brother Gaius observed all this. He was twenty-one when his brother was murdered. He spent the next decade building political support, and in 123 BCE, he was elected tribune. If the Senate thought killing Tiberius would end reform politics, they were wrong. Gaius was more radical, more talented, and more dangerous than his brother had been.

Gaius Gracchus moved fast. First, he revived the land commission and pushed even harder for redistribution. Then he proposed founding new colonies, not just in Italy but overseas, giving poor Romans land and a chance to start over somewhere new.

He also passed a grain law. The state would sell grain at subsidized prices, making food affordable for the poor. Critics called it blatant vote-buying. Supporters said it prevented starvation and mass unrest. Either way, it was the start of Rome's first permanent grain dole—the beginning of the "bread" in "bread and circuses."

Gaius didn't stop there. He took on the court system as well. At the time, senators judged other senators in extortion trials, essentially letting the elite police themselves. Gaius shifted jury duty to the equestrian class, breaking the Senate's grip on the courts and gaining a powerful new base of support.

He went even further than his brother, proposing that Italy's allies be granted full Roman citizenship. These men made up half of Rome's army but had no political rights. It was a bold move, and it made him a lot of enemies.

Gaius was elected tribune for 122 BCE as well; it seems the law prohibiting consecutive terms was being ignored by this point. He dominated Roman politics. The Senate couldn't stop him through legal means, and his legislation passed.

Then the Senate found his weakness: the citizenship proposal. Roman citizens in the lower classes didn't want to share citizenship with Italians. More citizens meant more competition for land, grain subsidies, and jobs.

A rival tribune, Marcus Livius Drusus, proposed even more generous land and colonial plans specifically for Roman citizens, not Italians. This split Gaius's coalition, and his citizenship proposal failed.

In 121 BCE, Gaius ran for tribune a third time and lost. Without the tribunate's legal protections, he was vulnerable. The Senate declared a *senatus consultum ultimum* (the "final decree of the Senate" that granted the consuls emergency authority to defend the state by whatever means they deemed necessary). This wasn't a law, but it essentially gave magistrates a shield against prosecution for actions they might take to restore order.

The consul Lucius Opimius raised an armed force and hunted down Gaius and his supporters. Gaius tried to escape across the Tiber but was cornered. He ordered his slave to kill him rather than let him be captured. According to ancient sources, about three thousand of his supporters were killed in the violence. Opimius offered to pay gold for Gaius's head—literally, the head's weight in gold. Someone brought it to him, allegedly with the brain removed and replaced with lead to increase the weight. The Senate rewarded Opimius by allowing him to build a temple to Concord—"harmony"—in the Forum on the site of the massacre. It was supposed to signal reconciliation. Instead, it looked like a monument to bloodshed.

The Gracchi brothers had tried to save the Roman Republic by addressing the economic crisis. They showed that popular tribunes could bypass the Senate by appealing directly to the people. Both were dead, and their reforms were partially rolled back, but the precedent had been set: political disputes could be settled with violence.

**Marius and Sulla: When Generals Started Caring More About Their Troops Than the State**

The generation after the Gracchi saw the rise of a new type of Roman politician: the military strongman whose power base was his army rather than his political connections.

Gaius Marius was a "new man," someone whose family had never held the consulship before. He came from the equestrian class in the town of Arpinum, not from Rome's aristocratic families. This made him an outsider in a political system dominated by established dynasties. Marius compensated with his military talent and political ruthlessness.

Marius made his reputation in North Africa fighting a war against Jugurtha, the king of Numidia (modern Algeria). The war had dragged on for years under incompetent commanders. Marius served as legate (similar to a modern general) under Quintus Caecilius Metellus, although he did most of the actual work. He returned to Rome and successfully ran for consul in 107 BCE by claiming that his aristocratic commander was prolonging the war through incompetence.

Attacking a superior officer and running for consul as a new man against senatorial opposition was politically radical. But Marius won by appealing directly to the people, promising to end the war quickly if given command.

Once consul, Marius did something radical: he opened military service to the poorest citizens. Previously, only citizens who owned property could serve. The idea was that property owners had a stake in defending Rome. Marius said forget that. Now, the *capite censi* (literally "head count," the poorest citizens who owned nothing) could join. Rome's army went from a citizen militia to a professional military.

Why would Gaius Marius do this? Rome needed bodies. Wars in Africa and Spain required soldiers, but the pool of property-owning citizens kept shrinking. Marius's reform tapped into thousands of unemployed men desperate for steady pay, three meals a day, and maybe some loot.

The state provided armor, weapons, and shields now. Men no longer had to show up with their own equipment. Soldiers served for years, sometimes decades, developing real professional skills. Roman legions became more effective fighting forces as a result. Veterans formed their own social class. These were career soldiers who saw military service as a job, not a civic duty.

But here's the catch: professional soldiers were loyal to their generals, not to Rome.

Think about it. The state didn't provide pensions. When your service ended, you had nothing. There was no farm to go back to because you never had one to begin with. Your only shot at security was if your general rewarded you with a land grant. So what if your general promised land and the Senate said no? You backed your general. Every time.

Marius won the war against Jugurtha with crucial help from his quaestor, Lucius Cornelius Sulla, who actually captured Jugurtha through diplomacy, something that Marius downplayed and Sulla resented. Then Germanic tribes, the Cimbri and Teutones, invaded from the north, threatening Italy itself. Marius was elected consul five years in a row, from 104 to 100 BCE, breaking the rule that said no one could hold the office twice within ten years. But Rome was scared, and Marius was their war hero.

Marius destroyed the Germanic invaders in two massive battles: Aquae Sextiae in 102 BCE and Vercellae in 101 BCE. He became Rome's savior and most popular general. He used his popularity to push through land grants for his veterans despite senatorial opposition. The precedent was set. Successful generals could demand rewards for their troops and use political pressure or the threat of military force to get them.

But then Marius made a political miscalculation. In 100 BCE, during his sixth consulship, he allied with violent populist politicians Lucius Appuleius Saturninus and Gaius Servilius Glaucia, who used gangs to intimidate opponents and disrupt voting. When their tactics became too extreme, the Senate issued the *senatus consultum ultimum* against them. Marius, as consul, was ordered to suppress his own allies. He did, killing Saturninus and Glaucia, but this destroyed his political base. Marius became isolated. He was too radical for conservatives and seen as too willing to betray allies for populists.

He spent the next decade mostly retired from politics, bitter and waiting for another opportunity to reclaim power. That opportunity came from an unexpected source: a war against Rome's Italian allies.

Rome's Italian allies had been asking for Roman citizenship for decades. They provided half of Rome's soldiers but couldn't vote or hold office. After Gaius Gracchus's citizenship proposal failed in 122 BCE, resentment festered. In 91 BCE, the tribune Marcus Livius Drusus proposed a new citizenship law. When Drusus was assassinated (almost certainly by senatorial opponents), the Italians revolted.

The Social War (91-88 BCE)—named from *socii*, Latin for "allies"—was Rome's most dangerous conflict since Hannibal had invaded. The Italians weren't barbarians or foreigners. They were Latins, Samnites, and other Italic peoples who had fought alongside Rome for centuries. They knew Roman military tactics intimately because they'd served in Roman armies. They created their own confederation, called Italia, with a capital at Corfinium (renamed Italica). They minted their own coins showing an Italian bull goring a Roman wolf, elected their own magistrates, and raised armies using Roman organizational structures.

The Italians weren't trying to destroy Rome. They wanted to be Romans. They wanted citizenship, voting rights, and legal equality. The war was about inclusion, not conquest. However, Rome's initial response was to fight rather than negotiate, viewing the revolt as treason.

The war was brutal and evenly matched. Both sides fought using Roman military tactics. Roman generals like Marius, Sulla, and Pompey Strabo (father of Pompey the Great) led campaigns. Tens of thousands died on both sides.

Rome gradually gained the upper hand militarily but recognized that crushing the revolt outright would be devastating. In 90 BCE, Rome passed the *Lex Julia,* granting citizenship to Italian communities that hadn't revolted or had laid down their arms. In 89 BCE, the *Lex Plautia Papiria* extended citizenship to individuals who registered with Roman authorities within sixty days. These laws essentially gave the Italians what they'd wanted.

The number of Roman citizens jumped from around 400,000 to over a million. The old line between Romans and Italians began to fade. Within a generation, nearly everyone in Italy would simply be Roman.

Then things got worse.

Mithridates VI, King of Pontus (in modern Turkey), invaded Roman territory in Asia Minor and massacred tens of thousands of Roman and Italian civilians. Rome needed to respond with force. The Senate assigned command of the war to the consul Lucius Cornelius Sulla, an aristocratic general from an old patrician family.

**A portrait of Sulla on a denarius.**[9]

Sulla had been Marius's subordinate in the Jugurthine War, serving as his quaestor. The two men had a complicated relationship. Sulla resented that Marius downplayed his role in capturing Jugurtha. Marius resented Sulla's aristocratic background and rising popularity. Now, in 88 BCE, Sulla had the prestigious eastern command, which Marius wanted.

Marius was in his seventies, but he was still ambitious. He allied with the tribune Publius Sulpicius Rufus, who proposed legislation transferring command of the Mithridatic War from Sulla to Marius. The proposal was blatantly unconstitutional (you couldn't just reassign a consul's command by vote), but it passed through the assembly.

Sulla responded in a way no Roman general had before. He marched on Rome with his army.

Six legions camped outside the city. Sulla told them that Marius was trying to steal their chance for glory and plunder in the east. The soldiers were loyal to Sulla; he was their commander, the man who would reward them with loot from Mithridates's wealthy kingdom. Ancient sources report that many of Sulla's officers refused to march on Rome, but the soldiers followed him.

Sulla's army entered Rome and fought street battles against Marius's supporters. This was civil war—Roman soldiers killing Roman citizens in Rome itself. It had never happened before. Publius Sulpicius Rufus was killed. Marius escaped to Africa. Sulla declared Marius and his supporters enemies of the state, seized their property, and repealed Sulpicius's laws.

Then Sulla made a crucial mistake. He left for the east to fight Mithridates, trusting that his political settlement would hold. It didn't. As soon as Sulla left Italy, Marius returned with an army. The consuls elected for 87 BCE, Gnaeus Octavius and Lucius Cornelius Cinna, split, with Cinna siding with Marius. Civil war broke out again.

Marius and Cinna captured Rome in 87 BCE. They unleashed a reign of terror against Sulla's supporters. Ancient sources describe massacres, proscriptions (official death lists), and the heads of murdered senators displayed in the Forum. Marius was elected consul for the seventh time, but he died in January 86 BCE, barely a month into his term. Cinna continued to control Rome in Sulla's absence.

Sulla spent years in the east defeating Mithridates and restoring Roman control of Greece and Asia Minor. He returned to Italy in 83 BCE with a hardened, loyal army and a determination to destroy his enemies. Young, talented officers flocked to him, including Pompey and Marcus Licinius

Crassus. From 83 to 81 BCE, Italy was consumed by civil war as Sulla crushed the Marian faction.

Sulla won. He had himself appointed dictator (an emergency office that granted absolute power for six months). Sulla held this role for three years. He instituted proscriptions on a scale that made Marius's massacres look restrained. Thousands were declared enemies of the state. Their property was confiscated, and they could be killed with impunity. Sulla's supporters enriched themselves by killing proscribed men and seizing their estates.

Sulla used his dictatorial power to reform the Roman Republic. He aimed to restore what he saw as the proper balance of power that had existed before the Gracchi brothers disrupted it. He weakened the tribunate by requiring tribunes to obtain Senate approval before proposing legislation and by making the tribunate a dead-end office; anyone who served as a tribune was barred from holding higher offices.

Sulla doubled the size of the Senate from three hundred to six hundred and packed it with his supporters. He gave the Senate back control of the courts and locked in a strict career ladder for politicians. There were minimum ages, mandatory waiting periods, and no repeating offices. Sulla also settled his veterans across Italy on confiscated land, creating a class of farmer-soldiers loyal to him and to the new order he'd imposed.

In 79 BCE, convinced he had saved the Roman Republic by restoring aristocratic rule, Sulla shocked everyone. He resigned. He gave up power, retired from public life, and died a year later. And not by assassination. He died in bed.

His so-called "reforms" collapsed almost immediately. Sulla had shown that a general with a loyal army could seize Rome, kill his enemies, and rule by force. However, in the decade after his death, Rome would face a different kind of threat, one that exposed the violence and fear upon which the entire Roman system was built.

### Spartacus: The Slave Rebellion That Exposed Rome's Greatest Fear

The Third Servile War (Spartacus's famous revolt) wasn't Rome's first major slave rebellion. Sicily had erupted in revolt twice before, from 135 to 132 BCE and from 104 to 100 BCE, when tens of thousands of slaves revolted and seized cities. They held out for years before Rome crushed them. But those rebellions happened on an island, far from Rome itself. Spartacus's rebellion was different. It happened in Italy.

In 73 BCE, about seventy gladiators escaped from a training school in Capua, south of Rome. Their leader was Spartacus, a Thracian (from modern Bulgaria) who'd been enslaved and forced to fight as a gladiator. The escapees seized weapons from a nearby town, fortified themselves on Mount Vesuvius, and began raiding the surrounding countryside.

Rome sent a small force to crush what looked like a minor disturbance. Spartacus destroyed it. More slaves, agricultural workers, household servants, and anyone who could escape fled to join him. Within months, Spartacus commanded thousands of escaped slaves. Ancient sources claim his army eventually swelled to around seventy thousand.

This scared Rome badly. Slaves made up perhaps a third of Italy's population. If they could organize and fight effectively, they threatened the entire social order. Wealthy Romans who owned large numbers of slaves had reason to worry. The people working their estates knew their routines, had access to tools and weapons, and might flee to join the rebellion.

Rome sent more armies. Spartacus won several major victories, defeating multiple Roman commanders. He wasn't just lucky; he was a capable leader. He equipped his forces with captured Roman weapons and organized them using disciplined tactics. He defeated praetors and even consuls. He marched his army the length of Italy, from south to north, winning engagement after engagement.

Spartacus's goal remains debated. Ancient sources claim he wanted to lead his followers over the Alps and bring them back to their homelands. But when his army reached northern Italy in 72 BCE, they turned back south. Maybe Spartacus lost control of his forces. Maybe his followers wanted to keep plundering Italy. Maybe he never intended to leave. We don't know.

What's clear is that by 71 BCE, Spartacus's army was still in southern Italy, and Rome had finally sent someone competent to deal with them: Marcus Licinius Crassus.

Crassus was Rome's richest man, but he lacked military glory, the one thing Roman politics required for the highest offices. Defeating Spartacus was his chance. The Senate gave him eight legions, over forty thousand soldiers. This time, Rome wasn't taking chances.

Crassus was ruthless. When some of his soldiers fled from battle, he revived the ancient punishment of decimation, in which every tenth man was beaten to death by his fellow soldiers. He wanted his own troops to fear him more than they feared the enemy.

Crassus trapped Spartacus in the toe of Italy, building a wall across the peninsula to contain the slave army. Spartacus broke through and marched north again, but Crassus pursued. In 71 BCE, the armies met in Lucania. The battle was brutal. According to ancient sources, Spartacus tried to fight his way to Crassus himself but was cut down. His body was never identified among the thousands of corpses.

The slave army broke and fled. Roman cavalry hunted down the survivors. Ancient sources report that 6,000 captured slaves were crucified along the Appian Way from Capua to Rome, 120 miles of road, their bodies left hanging as a warning that this was what happened to slaves who rebelled.

Crassus broke the rebellion. But Pompey, returning from Spain, intercepted and killed five thousand fleeing slaves. Pompey then sent dispatches to Rome claiming he'd finished the war, infuriating Crassus, who'd done the actual fighting. Both men wanted consulships. The question of who deserved credit for ending the rebellion became a bitter rivalry that would shape Roman politics for the next decade.

The Spartacus rebellion exposed something Romans didn't like to think about: their entire civilization rested on enslaving millions of people by force. Those people didn't accept their enslavement passively. They would fight for freedom if given the chance. Rome's response was to make the consequences of rebellion so terrifying that slaves would never dare try again.

It worked. For the next several centuries, no slave rebellion in Italy would come close to Spartacus's success. The crucified bodies along the Appian Way made sure of that.

### The First Triumvirate: Caesar, Pompey, and Crassus—The Three-Way Tug of War

The generation after Sulla produced three men who would dominate Roman politics and ultimately destroy the Roman Republic: Pompey, Crassus, and Julius Caesar.

Gnaeus Pompeius Magnus, better known as Pompey the Great, earned his reputation at a young age. At twenty-three, he raised legions to support Sulla in the civil war. Sulla called him "the Great" (*Magnus*) sarcastically—the young man was arrogant—but Pompey adopted the nickname seriously. After Sulla's death, Pompey received extraordinary commands to suppress rebellions in Sicily, Africa, and Spain. He defeated the Sertorian rebellion in Spain (though his subordinate actually killed

Sertorius). On his return to Italy in 71 BCE, Pompey mopped up the remnants of Spartacus's slave rebellion, which Marcus Licinius Crassus had already defeated, then claimed credit for ending the whole affair.

Marcus Licinius Crassus was Rome's richest man. He made his fortune through political connections, real estate speculation (ancient sources describe him owning a private fire brigade that would negotiate prices while buildings burned), and the purchase of property from proscribed men during Sulla's dictatorship.

In 70 BCE, Pompey and Crassus ran for consul together. They both lacked the constitutional qualifications. Pompey had never held the required lower offices, and both were below the minimum age. They pressured the Senate to waive the requirements. They won the election and used their consulship to undo Sulla's constitutional reforms, restoring the tribunate's powers and opening the courts to equestrians. After their consulship, they became rivals.

Pompey received command of a war against Mediterranean pirates, who were disrupting grain shipments and threatening Rome's food supply. The *Lex Gabinia* in 67 BCE granted Pompey supreme command over the entire Mediterranean and its coasts, with unlimited resources. Pompey cleared the seas of pirates in three months through a massive, coordinated campaign. This achievement greatly enhanced his reputation across Rome.

Then, in 66 BCE, the *Lex Manilia* transferred command of the ongoing war against Mithridates to Pompey. Mithridates VI of Pontus (a kingdom in modern Turkey) had been fighting Rome on and off since 88 BCE, when he'd massacred tens of thousands of Roman and Italian civilians in Asia Minor. Sulla had fought him, and then Lucullus—a capable general who'd been winning steadily for years—commanded the war through the 70s BCE. But Lucullus's troops were exhausted and restive after years of hard campaigning, and Pompey's political allies claimed only Pompey could finish the job.

Pompey defeated Mithridates, who committed suicide to avoid capture. He conquered Syria, reorganized the east, and returned to Italy in 62 BCE as Rome's most successful general, having expanded Roman territory across the eastern Mediterranean.

Pompey expected the Senate to approve his settlements in the east and grant land to his veterans. The Senate, led by Cato the Younger (great-grandson of Cato the Elder), refused. They were not going to let Pompey dictate terms simply because he commanded legions. They blocked his legislation and humiliated him politically.

This drove Pompey to join an alliance with two men who also had grievances against the Senate: Marcus Licinius Crassus and a rising politician named Gaius Julius Caesar.

Julius Caesar came from an ancient patrician family; the Julii claimed descent from the goddess Venus. But they had fallen on hard times. Caesar grew up during the Marian-Sullan civil wars. His aunt Julia was actually married to Marius. His first wife, Cornelia, was the daughter of Cinna (who sided with Marius during the war). When Sulla demanded that Caesar divorce Cornelia, Caesar refused and went into hiding. Sulla's allies pressured him to pardon Caesar, allegedly saying, "You win, but I'm telling you that this boy will destroy everything we've fought for. There are many Mariuses in him."

Caesar climbed the *cursus honorum* through a combination of charm, political skill, and massive debt. He borrowed enormous sums to fund public games, build patronage networks through lavish spending, and create political connections. By 59 BCE, he was deeply in debt to Crassus and needed a lucrative provincial command to restore his finances. He also wanted military glory to match Pompey's.

In 60 BCE, these three men formed a private political alliance known as the First Triumvirate. It was not an official alliance; it was more like an agreement that they would support one another's interests against senatorial opposition. Pompey wanted his eastern settlements ratified and land for his veterans. Crassus wanted tax relief for the equestrian companies with which he was connected. Caesar wanted the consulship for 59 BCE and then a military command.

The alliance worked. Caesar was elected consul for 59 BCE. He pushed through Pompey's legislation by intimidation and violence, ignoring his co-consul Marcus Calpurnius Bibulus, who tried to obstruct him. Caesar then secured command of Cisalpine Gaul (northern Italy) and Transalpine Gaul (southern France) for five years. He commanded four legions. This gave him the military opportunity he needed.

To cement the alliance, Pompey married Caesar's daughter Julia, despite being twenty-three years older than she was. Political marriages were normal in Rome, but ancient sources suggest this one was genuinely affectionate.

Caesar left for Gaul in 58 BCE. Over the next nine years, he would conquer territory roughly the size of modern France and Belgium, build an army of battle-hardened veterans loyal to him personally, and become the most famous general in Rome. He would also become too powerful for the Senate to control.

That story—the Gallic Wars, the civil war, and Caesar's transformation of Rome—would reshape the Roman world forever. But it belongs to the next chapter.

# Chapter 5: Julius Caesar: The Man, The Myth, The Knife

## The Conquest of Gaul: How Caesar Built His Brand and His Army

Julius Caesar left Rome in 58 BCE as a politician drowning in debt. He came back nine years later as the most famous general in the Mediterranean world, commanding an army of battle-hardened veterans who'd follow him anywhere. The Gallic Wars transformed Caesar from a talented but broke senator into the man who would destroy the Roman Republic.

Caesar's governorship gave him control of Cisalpine Gaul (northern Italy) and Transalpine Gaul (southern France), plus authority over nearby territories. He had four legions and permission to conduct military operations. What he didn't have was a convenient enemy or an obvious war to fight. So Caesar did what Caesar did best: he created his own opportunities.

His first opportunity came immediately. The Helvetii, a Celtic tribe from modern Switzerland, decided to migrate westward across Gaul. They weren't invading Roman territory. They weren't attacking Rome's allies. They just wanted to move. But Caesar claimed their migration threatened Roman interests. What if Germanic tribes filled the vacuum they left? He intercepted the Helvetii with his legions, fought a battle near Bibracte, and forced them home. Caesar's account claims he killed or captured most of the 368,000 Helvetii who'd started the journey. Modern historians think he inflated that number massively, but the point was still made. Caesar was in charge now.

Next came Ariovistus, a Germanic chieftain who'd crossed the Rhine into Gaul with his warriors. Gallic tribes asked Caesar for help, and Caesar was happy to oblige. He fought Ariovistus and drove him back across the Rhine. Caesar spun this as defending Gaul from Germanic invasion. In reality, he was establishing that Rome—meaning Caesar—now ran things in Gaul.

Then Caesar turned to the Belgic tribes in northern Gaul. These were fierce warriors who alarmed him with their military prowess. He campaigned against them, defeating the Nervii in a hard-fought battle in which his legion nearly broke before Caesar personally rallied his troops.

According to Caesar's account, the battle against the Nervii was one of his closest calls. The Nervii waited until Caesar's legions were divided and then launched a surprise attack. They moved so fast that Roman soldiers barely had time to arm themselves. The battle devolved into chaos. One Roman legion was surrounded and being cut to pieces. Caesar's own headquarters was under attack. Roman standards were falling, a catastrophe that would signal complete defeat.

In his *Commentarii de Bello Gallico* (*Commentaries on the Gallic War*), Caesar describes grabbing a shield from a soldier in the rear ranks and pushing forward to the front line, calling out centurions by name and urging the ranks to spread out so they had room to use their swords. Whether this personal intervention happened exactly as Caesar described or was embellished for dramatic effect, the story served its purpose by portraying Caesar as the brave commander who personally turned near-defeat into victory through courage and tactical awareness.

Then the Tenth Legion arrived from the rear and crashed into the Nerviis' flank. The Nervii fought to almost total annihilation, according to ancient sources.

Over the next few years, Caesar systematically brought Gaul under Roman control. He fought the Veneti, a coastal tribe with a powerful navy that controlled trade along the Atlantic coast. The Veneti built heavy vessels with leather sails and high hulls that made them difficult to ram. Caesar had his engineers build Roman ships and adapt grappling hooks on long poles to cut the Veneti's rigging. Without their sails, Veneti ships became helpless, and Roman boarding tactics secured victory. Caesar punished the Veneti harshly. He executed their entire council of elders and sold the rest of the tribe into slavery. The severity was deliberate, a warning to other tribes not to resist.

He crossed the Rhine, constructing a bridge in ten days, according to his account, to raid Germanic territory and demonstrate Roman power. He invaded Britain twice, in 55 and 54 BCE. These expeditions beyond established Roman frontiers led the Romans to describe them as crossing the "Ocean," their term for seas beyond the Mediterranean. The British expeditions achieved little in terms of lasting conquest but generated enormous publicity in Rome, where people were fascinated by reports of this mysterious island at the edge of the known world.

An illustration of the Romans landing in Britain.[10]

The wars weren't easy. Gallic warriors were formidable. They were big, strong, experienced fighters who wielded long swords and shields and favored shock tactics. Celtic culture valued individual martial prowess, and Gallic nobles were raised from birth to be warriors. But the Gauls fought as tribal militias. Each tribe was independent and often feuding with its neighbors. Caesar exploited these divisions ruthlessly, allying with some tribes and keeping Gaul divided and conquerable.

Roman military discipline gave Caesar crucial advantages. His legions could march farther, build faster, and fight in coordinated formations that Gallic war bands couldn't match. Roman engineering allowed Caesar to build camps, bridges, and siege works that amazed his enemies. Roman logistics enabled sustained campaigns that would have exhausted tribal forces. And Caesar himself was a talented commander. He was quick to recognize opportunities, willing to take risks, and skilled at motivating his soldiers.

But the conquest nearly came undone in 52 BCE, when Vercingetorix, a young Gallic nobleman, achieved what no one else had managed: he united most of Gaul against Rome.

Vercingetorix was brilliant. Instead of facing Caesar in pitched battles, where Roman discipline dominated, he used scorched-earth tactics, burning towns and crops to deny Caesar supplies. He employed guerrilla warfare, attacking Roman supply lines and foraging parties. He forced Caesar to chase him across Gaul while Roman soldiers grew hungry and exhausted.

The campaign culminated at Alesia, a fortified Gallic settlement where Vercingetorix concentrated his forces. Caesar besieged it, building eleven miles of fortifications to surround the town. However, a Gallic relief army approached to lift the siege. Caesar claimed the relief force numbered around 250,000 warriors, though modern historians regard this figure as logistically impossible. Regardless of the exact numbers, Caesar faced a substantial force outside Alesia while besieging Vercingetorix inside.

So, Caesar built a second line of fortifications facing outward. His men built fourteen miles of walls, ditches, and defensive positions to protect the Roman army from the relief force. His legions now sat between two enemies, one inside the walls and one outside, with fortifications on both sides.

The battle lasted days. The Gallic relief army attacked Caesar's outer defenses repeatedly. Vercingetorix tried to break out from inside. Caesar's legions fought on both fronts simultaneously. They were exhausted and outnumbered, but they held their positions. The relief army eventually broke and fled. Vercingetorix, seeing no hope of rescue, surrendered to save his people from starvation.

Caesar kept Vercingetorix imprisoned for six years. Ancient sources report that he was then strangled during Caesar's triumph (a victory parade) in 46 BCE.

The Gallic Wars were over. Caesar had conquered territory roughly the size of modern France and Belgium. The cost was staggering. Ancient writers like Plutarch reported Caesar's claims of one million Gauls killed and one million enslaved, though modern historians suggest these figures include combat deaths, massacres, famine caused by scorched-earth tactics and sieges, and displacement rather than direct battlefield casualties alone. Regardless of precise numbers, the wars devastated Gaul's population. Many of those who remained were sold into slavery. Ancient sources report that the wars enriched Caesar personally through plundering Gallic temples, selling captives, and extracting tribute. It made him wealthy enough to pay off his debts and fund future political campaigns.

More importantly, Caesar created an army. Ten legions of veterans had fought with him for nearly a decade. They trusted his leadership, had been rewarded with plunder and bonuses, and expected Caesar to secure land grants when they retired. They would follow him anywhere—even across the Rubicon into Italy against the Senate's authority.

Caesar also created something else. His *Commentarii de Bello Gallico—Commentaries on the Gallic War*—was widely admired by educated Romans for its clear, direct Latin prose and proved highly effective as political communication. Written in the third person (Caesar always referred to himself as "Caesar" rather than "I"), they presented his campaigns as necessary defensive actions taken by a dutiful Roman general protecting Rome's interests. They made Caesar famous not just as a general but as a writer. By the time he crossed the Rubicon, Caesar was arguably the most famous man in Rome.

### Crossing the Rubicon: The Point of No Return and the End of the Republic

By 50 BCE, Caesar's enemies in Rome knew they had a problem. Caesar was immensely popular. His *Commentarii* were bestsellers and were being read aloud in the Forum. His military reputation rivaled Pompey's. His wealth was enormous. His army was loyal and battle-hardened. If Caesar returned to Rome with his power intact, he would dominate Roman politics for decades.

The Senate, led by conservatives like Cato the Younger, decided to neutralize Caesar legally. Roman governors lost their authority upon entering Italy. Once Caesar crossed into Italy, he'd be just another citizen, vulnerable to prosecution. The charges might not stick, but the trial would humiliate Caesar and wreck his political career.

Caesar knew this. His solution? Run for consul while still holding his provincial command. He would stay in office continuously. Then, as consul, he would protect himself and reward his veterans with land.

The Senate said no. Caesar had to give up his command, come back as a private citizen, run for consul, and just trust that nobody would prosecute him. Caesar countered that he should be allowed to run without returning to Rome, keeping his command until he could take office. The Senate refused again.

Both sides were playing chicken. The Senate wanted Caesar vulnerable. Caesar wanted guarantees. Neither trusted the other. Both had good reasons not to.

By January 49 BCE, negotiations had collapsed. The Senate passed the *senatus consultum ultimum*, an emergency decree that effectively instructed the consuls to do whatever it took to defend the state. In other words, the consuls had to stop Caesar by force if necessary. The tribunes who supported Caesar, Mark Antony and Quintus Cassius Longinus, fled Rome immediately. They disguised themselves, possibly as slaves, and raced north to Caesar's camp.

Caesar now had his propaganda victory. Tribunes who were supposed to be sacred and untouchable were fleeing Rome? Caesar could present this as persecution, as the Senate driving out the people's representatives. He would march on Rome not as a rebel but as a defender of Roman rights against senatorial tyranny.

On January 10th, 49 BCE, Caesar stood at the Rubicon River, a small stream marking the boundary between his province of Cisalpine Gaul and Italy proper. Roman law strictly forbade generals from bringing armies into Italy without the Senate's permission. Crossing with his legions would be rebellion.

According to ancient sources, Caesar hesitated. He knew that crossing meant civil war. Once across, there was no peaceful solution. If he won, he would be Rome's master. If he lost, he would be executed as a traitor.

Then Caesar said, "Alea iacta est" ("The die is cast"), and crossed with the Thirteenth Legion.

The phrase became immortal. It captured the moment when Caesar chose war over submission, when the Roman Republic's last hope for a peaceful resolution died, and when the course was set toward dictatorship and, eventually, empire. The die was cast. The outcome was now in the hands of fate and force.

**Julius Caesar.**[11]

Caesar moved fast. He marched south through Italy, not plundering like an invader but presenting himself as a liberator defending the people's rights. Many towns opened their gates without resistance. Caesar's mercy was tactical. He pardoned enemies, spared cities that surrendered, and portrayed himself as reluctant to spill Roman blood. This contrasted sharply with memories of Sulla's brutality, making Caesar appear reasonable.

Pompey and the senatorial forces were unprepared. They had expected Caesar to negotiate or back down. Instead, he moved with shocking speed. Pompey couldn't raise enough troops to defend Italy. On the Senate's advice, he evacuated to Greece, taking his legions and many senators with him. Pompey's strategy was to control the eastern provinces, build an overwhelming force, then invade Italy and crush Caesar with superior numbers.

Caesar entered Rome unopposed in March 49 BCE. He had conquered Italy in sixty days without fighting a major battle. The Senate had fled. Republican institutions continued to function formally, though real political power had shifted decisively to Caesar.

However, the civil war was just beginning. Pompey commanded the east. Senators loyal to the Roman Republic's traditions rallied to his standard. Spain's legions remained uncertain. North Africa was contested. The Mediterranean was split between Caesar's faction and Pompey's coalition. For the next four years, Romans would kill Romans in battles across three continents.

### Dictator for Life: Caesar's Reforms and the Ego That Got Him Killed

Caesar spent the years 49 to 45 BCE fighting a civil war on multiple fronts. He defeated Pompey's forces in Spain. He then chased Pompey to Greece and beat him at Pharsalus in 48 BCE.

Pharsalus was the decisive battle of the civil war. Pompey commanded about forty-five thousand infantry and seven thousand cavalry—nearly double Caesar's forces. Pompey's strategy was to use his cavalry superiority to envelop Caesar's right flank and then roll up his entire line. It should have worked. Pompey's cavalry was experienced, his army was larger, and he held the defensive position.

But Caesar anticipated the cavalry attack. He secretly positioned six cohorts (about three thousand men) behind his right wing with orders to target the cavalry specifically. His men were to thrust their javelins upward at the riders' faces rather than throwing them. When Pompey's cavalry charged, these cohorts emerged and attacked with disciplined jabbing motions. The cavalry, unused to infantry aggressively stabbing at their faces, panicked and fled. Caesar's cavalry pursued, then swept around and struck Pompey's infantry from behind.

Pompey's larger army collapsed. Ancient sources report that about fifteen thousand of Pompey's men died, and twenty-four thousand surrendered. Caesar claimed his own casualties were around two hundred, a figure that strains credibility in a battle involving nearly seventy thousand men and likely represents significant underreporting.

Regardless of exact numbers, the battle was very much one-sided. Pompey fled the battlefield, abandoning his army. Caesar's veterans had crushed a much larger force through superior tactics and discipline. Caesar famously commented, "They would have it so," meaning the senatorial faction had forced this battle and suffered the consequences.

Pompey fled to Egypt. The young pharaoh, Ptolemy XIII, had him murdered, probably hoping to score points with Caesar. When Caesar arrived in Alexandria, someone handed him Pompey's head. Caesar supposedly wept. Maybe the tears were real—Pompey had been his son-in-law and ally before becoming his enemy. Maybe they were theater. Either way, they fit Caesar's carefully cultivated image. This merciful victor was saddened by Roman bloodshed.

Caesar spent the winter of 48–47 BCE in Egypt, becoming entangled in Egyptian politics and beginning his famous affair with Cleopatra VII. He backed Cleopatra against her brother Ptolemy in Egypt's civil war. When Caesar left, Cleopatra was in charge, pregnant with Caesar's son, and Egypt was firmly in Rome's—or rather, Caesar's—orbit.

This mattered politically beyond the scandal. Egypt was the richest kingdom in the Mediterranean. It had grain that could feed Rome and gold that made Rome's treasury look pathetic. By making Cleopatra his ally and lover, Caesar controlled Egypt's resources without bothering to ask the Senate. Cleopatra later moved to Rome, living in Caesar's villa across the Tiber. A foreign queen openly living as Caesar's mistress while he was still married horrified conservative Romans. Rumors spread that Caesar planned to marry her, make their son his heir, and maybe even move Rome's capital to Alexandria. This was probably not true, but the rumors fed fears that Caesar wanted to be an eastern-style king, not a Roman magistrate.

Caesar then defeated Pharnaces, King of Pontus, in a brief campaign that produced his famous dispatch, "Veni, vidi, vici" ("I came, I saw, I conquered"). These three words capture Caesar's military genius and his talent for self-promotion.

In 46 BCE, Caesar crushed the remaining senatorial forces in North Africa at Thapsus. In 45 BCE, he destroyed the last resistance at Munda in Spain, where Pompey's sons led a desperate final stand. The civil war was over. Caesar had won. The Senate was cowed. His opponents were dead, exiled, or pardoned and humiliated.

Caesar held multiple dictatorships during these years. They were technically legal emergency positions, but they stretched far beyond their traditional bounds. After Munda, the Senate granted Caesar the dictatorship for ten years. Then, in 44 BCE, they made him *dictator perpetuo*, or dictator for life. This was unprecedented. The dictatorship was supposed to be a six-month emergency office. Making it permanent destroyed the pretense that Caesar's power was temporary.

Caesar used his power to push through massive reforms. Some were genuinely beneficial to Rome. Others enhanced his own authority. All of them reflected Caesar's brilliance, ambition, and dangerous confidence that he knew what Rome needed better than anyone else.

He reformed the calendar, creating what we now call the Julian calendar, with 365 days, 12 months, and leap years. The old Roman calendar had fallen hopelessly out of sync with the seasons because priests manipulated it for political purposes. Caesar fixed it with the help of Greek astronomers. The result was so effective that we still use a version of it today, more than two thousand years later.

Ancient sources report that he expanded the Senate to nine hundred members, packing it with his supporters. This diluted the old senatorial elite's power and ensured Caesar had a compliant Senate. However, it also insulted the aristocracy by elevating men they considered unworthy.

He founded colonies for his veterans and the urban poor. Ancient sources and modern reconstructions suggest he settled perhaps eighty thousand Romans in new communities across the Mediterranean. This relieved pressure on Rome's grain supply and rewarded his soldiers with land.

Caesar also reformed debt laws, helping debtors without completely alienating creditors. He planned massive public works, draining marshes, building a new Forum, and expanding Rome's infrastructure. Some of these projects continued after his death. He granted citizenship more liberally, extending it to communities in Gaul and Spain. This expanded Rome's citizen body and created loyalty to Caesar.

But Caesar also accepted honors that alarmed traditionalists. Ancient sources describe the Senate voting for him to have a golden throne, placing his image on coins (the first living Roman so honored), and renaming the month Quintilis as Julius (our July). They granted him the right to wear a laurel wreath constantly, which conveniently covered his baldness, something Caesar was reportedly vain about. They gave him honors usually reserved for gods, including temples, priests, and religious rituals in his name. Modern scholars debate the timing and political significance of these honors, but it was clear that Caesar was receiving unprecedented recognition.

Caesar accepted all of this. Whether he believed he deserved divine honors or simply couldn't resist the flattery is impossible to know. However, to many Romans, it seemed Caesar wanted to be king or, worse, to be worshiped as a god.

The word "king" (*rex*) was still toxic in Rome. Romans had been taught for five hundred years to hate kings. When someone in a crowd reportedly called Caesar "rex," Caesar immediately replied, "I am Caesar, not rex." When Mark Antony offered Caesar a royal diadem at the Lupercalia festival in February 44 BCE, Caesar publicly refused it twice, for emphasis. Yet the rumors persisted. Why would Antony offer it if Caesar didn't want it? Was Caesar testing public reaction? Was it political theater designed to make him appear humble while preparing the public to accept him as king?

Caesar's veterans loved him. The common people appreciated his generosity and reforms. But senators, even those who had supported him, were becoming increasingly alarmed. Caesar was acting like a monarch. He made decisions unilaterally. He bypassed the Senate. He appointed magistrates rather than allowing elections. He did not consult the great aristocratic families. He treated the Senate like a rubber stamp.

And Caesar was planning to leave Rome again, this time for a massive military expedition against Parthia. He wanted to avenge Crassus's defeat at Carrhae. Caesar would be gone for years campaigning in the east while Rome waited for his return. Such a victory would make Caesar even more powerful, as he would be the conqueror of Rome's only remaining rival.

Some senators decided that Caesar had to die, not for personal reasons—many had been pardoned by him, promoted by him, or enriched by him—but for the republic. They convinced themselves that killing Caesar would allow Rome to return to its traditional government.

They were senators, many from the old aristocracy. They believed in the Roman Republic's values of liberty, shared power, and the rule of law. And they believed that one man, no matter how talented, should not rule Rome. Caesar had destroyed the Roman Republic's system. In their minds, the only way to restore it was to kill him.

## The Ides of March: Why His "Friends" Thought They Were Saving Rome by Murdering Him

The conspiracy formed slowly and carefully. Around sixty senators eventually joined, though only a few knew all the details. The ringleaders were Gaius Cassius Longinus and Marcus Junius Brutus.

Recruiting conspirators was a delicate process. Each man had to be absolutely trusted; one informant could expose the entire plot and get everyone executed. The conspirators were recruited primarily from the Senate's ranks, focusing on men who had fought for Pompey or the

Republican cause but had been pardoned by Caesar. Many of these men owed their lives to Caesar's clemency, which made their betrayal more shocking but, in their minds, more principled. They were not killing Caesar out of personal hatred but from the belief that he threatened Rome's freedom. The conspirators called themselves the Liberatores (the Liberators).

Cassius was a competent military commander and longtime opponent of Caesar, though he had been pardoned and promoted after the Battle of Pharsalus. Ancient sources portray Cassius's motivations as a complex mix of personal animosity toward Caesar and genuine political conviction. He was driven by envy and ambition, as well as principle.

Brutus was different. He was Caesar's protégé. Ancient sources circulated rumors that he might have been Caesar's illegitimate son since Caesar had an affair with Brutus's mother, Servilia. Caesar favored Brutus, reportedly telling his guards, "Whatever Brutus wants, give it to him. And if he doesn't want it, don't force him." Brutus was descended from Lucius Junius Brutus, the legendary founder of the Roman Republic who expelled Rome's last king. That ancestry gave Brutus enormous symbolic importance. If Brutus joined the conspiracy, it would seem as if the Roman Republic's founder's descendant was saving Rome from a new king.

These men saw themselves as heroes defending Roman liberty against tyranny. They planned to kill Caesar publicly, in front of witnesses, to show they were acting openly for the good of Rome rather than sneaking around like common assassins. The murder would be tyrannicide—the righteous killing of a tyrant—not mere murder.

They chose March 15th (the Ides of March in the Roman calendar) when the Senate would meet in the Theatre of Pompey. Caesar would be in attendance. The conspirators would surround him and strike him down in front of the Senate. Then they would announce that Rome was free and that the Roman Republic had been restored.

In the days before the Ides of March, ancient historians recorded various omens, though whether these were real events or literary devices added later to heighten drama is unclear. A soothsayer supposedly warned Caesar to "beware the Ides of March." Lightning allegedly struck a statue. Sacrificial animals were said to have had no heart. Caesar's wife, Calpurnia, dreamed he was murdered and begged him not to go to the Senate meeting.

On the morning of March 15th, 44 BCE, Caesar almost did not go to the Senate. Calpurnia's dream troubled him. However, Decimus Brutus Albinus, one of the conspirators and one of Caesar's most trusted officers, came to Caesar's house and convinced him that canceling would appear weak. The Senate was waiting to grant Caesar new honors. How would it look if Caesar stayed home because of a bad dream?

So, Caesar went.

As he entered the theater, someone pressed a note into his hand; ancient sources say it listed the conspirators and their plot. Caesar tried to read it but was surrounded by senators eager to greet him. He never read the warning.

Caesar took his seat. The conspirators gathered around him under the pretense of petitioning him. Lucius Tillius Cimber approached first, asking Caesar to recall his exiled brother. When Caesar refused, Cimber grabbed Caesar's toga and pulled it down. This was the signal.

Casca struck first, stabbing Caesar in the neck. The wound was not fatal. Certain ancient accounts, including Suetonius and Plutarch, describe Caesar grabbing Casca's arm and stabbing back with his stylus, the pointed pen Romans used to write on wax tablets.

Then the other conspirators closed in. Twenty-three men stabbed Caesar repeatedly. Ancient sources say Caesar resisted at first, trying to fight off his attackers. But when he saw Brutus with a knife, Caesar allegedly said something. Some sources say he spoke in Greek: "Kai su, teknon?" ("You too, child?"). The famous Latin version, "Et tu, Brute?" comes from Shakespeare, not ancient sources. Whether Caesar said anything at all in his final moments, and if so, what remains uncertain. Eventually, Caesar stopped resisting. He pulled his toga over his head to die with dignity and fell at the base of Pompey's statue. The symbolism was perfect–Caesar died at the feet of his dead rival's memorial.

The conspirators stood there, covered in blood, expecting celebration. They thought the Senate would cheer. They thought the Roman people would praise them as liberators. They thought killing Caesar would restore the Roman Republic.

Instead, there was shocked silence, then panic. Senators fled the theater. The conspirators had no plan beyond the murder itself. They had killed Caesar but had not secured the support of his veterans. They had not prepared for what came next. They ran through the streets waving bloody daggers, shouting that Rome was free. But people hid in their houses. Rome was terrified, not celebrating.

The Liberators had made a catastrophic miscalculation. They thought Caesar was the problem, that removing him would restore the republic. They were wrong. Modern scholars see the Roman Republic's crisis as a structural failure. Sulla had shown that generals with loyal armies could seize Rome. Pompey and Crassus had shown that powerful individuals could bypass the Senate. Caesar had simply made these systemic problems impossible to ignore.

The Roman Republic's collapse stemmed not from one man's power but from the system's inability to withstand the stresses of empire. Rome's government had been designed for a small city-state, not a Mediterranean empire. The concentration of wealth in elite hands, the creation of professional armies loyal to commanders, and the impossibility of representing millions of citizens through assemblies in Rome could not be fixed by murdering Caesar.

Mark Antony, Caesar's ally and co-consul, seized control of Caesar's papers and funds. Caesar's deputy, Marcus Aemilius Lepidus, controlled troops in Rome. The conspirators had no army, no plan, and, within days, no support. Ancient sources such as Appian and Dio describe Caesar's funeral turning into a mob scene as Antony read Caesar's will, which left gardens and money to the Roman people. He also displayed Caesar's bloody toga. The crowd rioted, burned the conspirators' houses, and forced them to flee Rome.

**A bust believed to be Mark Antony.**[13]

And then there was Caesar's heir. Caesar's will named his eighteen-year-old grandnephew, Gaius Octavius, as his adopted son and heir. This teenager would change everything.

Caesar was dead. But Caesarism—rule by military strongmen claiming to represent the people against an ineffective Senate—would define Rome's future. The conspirators killed the man. They couldn't kill what he represented or reverse what he had revealed: that the Roman Republic couldn't survive as a world empire and that Roman politics would now be settled by armies, not votes.

# Chapter 6: Augustus and the Birth of the Empire

## Octavian: The Teenager Who Outplayed Everyone and Transformed Rome into an Empire

When Julius Caesar's will was read after his assassination in 44 BCE, it contained a surprise. Caesar had adopted his eighteen-year-old grandnephew, Gaius Octavius, as his son and heir. Most people in Rome had barely heard of this teenager. He was sickly, inexperienced, and came from Rome's elite but not from an established consular dynasty. He had no military experience. He controlled no legions. And he had no political base.

Mark Antony, Caesar's veteran co-consul who controlled Rome, laughed when he heard that this boy was claiming Caesar's inheritance. Cicero, the famous orator and senator, thought he could manipulate the young man, use him against Antony, and then discard him. The assassins who had killed Caesar dismissed Octavian as irrelevant.

They all underestimated him. Gaius Octavius would become Augustus Caesar, Rome's first emperor. He ruled for forty-one years and transformed the Roman state so completely that the republic would never return. He would outlive all his enemies, die peacefully in his bed, and be worshiped as a god. He was perhaps the most successful politician in Roman history—maybe in all of history.

A statue of Augustus.[18]

But in 44 BCE, he was just a teenager who had lost his adoptive father to assassination and was surrounded by powerful men who wanted to use him or destroy him.

Octavian's first move was brilliant. He took Caesar's name. He became Gaius Julius Caesar Octavianus. Names mattered in Rome. Caesar's name carried enormous prestige. Caesar's veterans saw Octavian as Caesar's heir who owed them what Caesar had promised. Caesar's political supporters saw continuity. Caesar's enemies saw a boy pretending to be Caesar, but he was a boy they could not ignore.

Octavian also had money. Caesar left him his personal fortune. Octavian used it expertly, paying bonuses to Caesar's veterans, funding games for the Roman people, and building political support through the time-honored method of strategic generosity.

However, Octavian faced a major obstacle: Mark Antony. Antony had been Caesar's right-hand man. He was a proven military commander and consul in 44 BCE. Antony controlled Rome politically and militarily. He expected to inherit Caesar's political legacy and become the dominant figure in Roman politics.

Antony treated Octavian with contempt, refusing to hand over Caesar's fortune, keeping Octavian waiting for hours during meetings, and publicly mocking him as a boy who owed everything to Caesar's name. This was a mistake. It pushed Octavian directly into an alliance with Antony's enemies.

The Senate, led by Cicero, saw an opportunity. They were terrified of Antony, whom they feared would become another Caesar, a military strongman dominating Rome. But they could not defeat Antony militarily. So, they decided to use Octavian. Cicero delivered speeches (later known as the *Philippics*) attacking Antony and praising Octavian. The Senate granted Octavian military command despite his age and lack of qualifications, hoping he would fight Antony on their behalf.

**A fresco by Cesare Maccari depicting Cicero speaking to the Senate.[14]**

Octavian accepted. He raised legions from Caesar's veterans, many of whom defected from Antony to serve Caesar's heir. In 43 BCE, Octavian marched north. Two battles were fought against Antony at Mutina (modern Modena). Antony was defeated and fled to Gaul. Both consuls, Aulus Hirtius and Gaius Vibius Pansa, died in the fighting, leaving Octavian in control of their legions. Later propaganda portrayed the nineteen-year-old Octavian as the brilliant commander who defeated Antony. The reality was messier, but the outcome was what mattered.

The Senate was thrilled. They had used Octavian to neutralize Antony. Now they could dispose of the teenager. They passed votes of thanks, denied Octavian the triumph he requested, and tried to strip him of his command. Ancient sources report that Cicero said Octavian should be "praised, honored, and disposed of" (the Latin verb *tollere* meaning both "to raise up" and "to eliminate").

Octavian learned that the Senate's promises were worthless. They would use him and then destroy him, just as they had tried to destroy Caesar. If he wanted to survive, he could not rely on senatorial goodwill.

So, at nineteen years old, Octavian marched on Rome with his legions. He demanded the consulship, backpay for his soldiers, and official recognition. The Senate, staring at armed legions, caved. Octavian became consul in August 43 BCE. He was the youngest consul in Roman history.

Octavian used his consulship to pass the *Lex Pedia,* which declared Caesar's assassins enemies of the state and created special courts to try them. This gave Octavian legal authority to hunt down Brutus, Cassius, and the other conspirators. It also made it clear that Octavian was Caesar's avenger, not the Senate's tool.

But Octavian still faced a problem: Antony. Antony had regrouped in Gaul, gathered legions, and allied with Marcus Aemilius Lepidus, Caesar's former deputy, who commanded troops in Spain and southern Gaul. Together, Antony and Lepidus controlled more military forces than Octavian did. Octavian needed to neutralize them or defeat them.

Instead, he did something unexpected: he allied with them.

### The Second Triumvirate: Thirteen Years of Proscriptions, Purges, and Power Politics

In November 43 BCE, Octavian, Antony, and Lepidus met near Bononia (modern Bologna) and formed an alliance. Unlike the First Triumvirate between Caesar, Pompey, and Crassus, which had been a private agreement, the Second Triumvirate was official. The three men had themselves appointed *triumviri rei publicae constituendae* ("three men for restoring the republic") with legal authority for five years. They essentially divided the Roman world among themselves. Antony took Gaul, Lepidus took Spain and southern Gaul, and Octavian took Africa and the islands.

But first, they needed money. They also needed to eliminate their enemies. So, they instituted proscriptions.

The proscriptions of 43–42 BCE were among the most brutal episodes in Roman history. The triumvirs drew up lists of political enemies. These could be senators, equestrians, or anyone who opposed them or whose wealth they wanted. Ancient sources such as Appian report that perhaps three hundred senators and two thousand equestrians were proscribed, though modern historians treat these as estimates rather than precise counts. The exact death toll is unknowable. Being proscribed meant you were declared an enemy of the state. Anyone could kill you and claim a reward. Your property was confiscated. Your family lost its legal protections.

The triumvirs were not killing for ideology. This was political murder for profit. Each triumvir had to sacrifice some of his own allies to satisfy the others' vengeance. Ancient sources describe the negotiations as callous bargaining. Antony wanted Cicero, Lepidus wanted certain senators, and Octavian needed to eliminate potential threats. They traded names like merchants trading goods.

The mechanics of proscription created a reign of terror. Lists were posted in the Forum. Men woke up to discover they were marked for death. Some tried to hide, while others fled. Few succeeded, as the ports were watched, and the roads were patrolled.

Cicero tried to flee Italy. Antony's soldiers caught him at his villa in December 43 BCE. They cut off his head and hands—the hands that had written the *Philippics*—and brought them to Rome. The head and hands were displayed in the Forum, where Cicero had delivered so many speeches.

Thousands died. The proscriptions terrorized Rome and enriched the triumvirs. By late 42 BCE, they had enough wealth to fund their armies and enough fear to prevent opposition.

With Italy secured and their enemies dead or in exile, the triumvirs turned their attention to the conspirators. Brutus and Cassius had fled east after Caesar's assassination and built an army in Greece and Asia Minor.

They controlled Rome's eastern provinces and commanded substantial military forces. If Octavian and Antony wanted to secure their power, they needed to destroy them.

In 42 BCE, Octavian and Antony crossed to Greece with their armies. Lepidus stayed in Italy to maintain control. At Philippi in Macedonia, the triumvirs' forces met the armies of Brutus and Cassius in two battles.

The first battle was indecisive. Brutus defeated Octavian's forces on one wing. Ancient sources suggest Octavian was sick and ineffective in battle. He was not present in his camp when it was overrun. But Antony crushed Cassius on the other wing. Cassius, seeing his camp captured and unaware that Brutus had prevailed on the opposite flank, committed suicide.

Three weeks later, Antony forced a second battle. Brutus's army, demoralized by Cassius's death and running low on supplies, fought but was decisively defeated. Brutus fled the battlefield and committed suicide rather than be captured. According to ancient accounts, Octavian treated Brutus's corpse with disrespect, sending the head to Rome to be thrown at the feet of Caesar's statue, though he honored other fallen enemies with a proper burial.

The Roman Republic's last defenders were dead. The triumvirs controlled the Roman world. But now they had to decide how to divide it and who would ultimately rule.

The settlement after Philippi gave Antony the East, the wealthy provinces of Greece, Asia Minor, Syria, and Egypt. Octavian received the West—Italy, Gaul, and Spain—and the difficult task of settling veterans, which required confiscating property and making enemies of displaced Italian landowners. Lepidus was sidelined to Africa, the least important territory. On paper, the division favored Antony. The East was richer, easier to govern, and further from Rome's political chaos. The West faced veteran land settlements, political instability, and the challenge of governing Italy itself.

Octavian's land confiscations triggered an immediate crisis. Italian landowners who lost property to veteran settlements were furious. Antony's brother, Lucius Antonius, and Antony's wife, Fulvia, exploited this anger, rallying opposition against Octavian. In 41 BCE, they raised an army and occupied Rome, claiming to represent Antony's interests and Italian property rights against Octavian's policies.

Octavian besieged them at Perusia (modern Perugia). The siege lasted months. When the city finally surrendered in early 40 BCE, Octavian displayed a ruthlessness he usually concealed behind political theater. Ancient sources report that he executed the city council and perhaps three hundred prominent citizens, allegedly declaring, "They must die" when they pleaded for mercy. He spared Lucius Antonius, Antony's brother, who was too important to kill, but the message was unmistakable. Opposition to Octavian would be crushed.

The Perusine War nearly triggered conflict between Octavian and Antony. However, both men realized that fighting each other would benefit only their enemies. In 40 BCE, they met at Brundisium and renewed their alliance. To seal the agreement, Antony married Octavian's sister Octavia. Antony's previous wife, Fulvia, had conveniently died not long before. The marriage was political, but ancient sources suggest Octavia was respected and dignified, making Antony's later abandonment of her for Cleopatra even more scandalous to Roman sensibilities.

Octavian and Antony faced yet another threat: Sextus Pompey, son of Pompey the Great. Sextus had fled to Sicily after the Battle of Philippi and built a powerful fleet. He controlled Sicily, Sardinia, and Corsica, which were key sources of Rome's grain supply. Sextus also offered refuge to proscribed men and escaped slaves, building a large military force. By blockading grain shipments, he could starve Rome and pressure the triumvirs.

For several years, Sextus functioned as a fourth power in the Roman world. The triumvirs tried bribing him and negotiating with him. Finally, in 39 BCE, they made peace through the Treaty of Misenum, which recognized Sextus's control of the islands in exchange for reopening the grain supply. But the peace did not last.

Between 38 and 36 BCE, Octavian fought a naval war against Sextus. The conflict went badly at first; Octavian lost ships to storms and suffered defeats in battle. However, Agrippa, Octavian's friend and most capable general, built a new fleet and trained crews in a specially constructed harbor. In 36 BCE, Agrippa defeated Sextus's fleet at Naulochus off Sicily. Sextus fled east to Antony's territories, where he was eventually captured and executed.

The defeat of Sextus gave Octavian control of the western Mediterranean and the crucial grain supply. It also provided a pretext to eliminate Lepidus. Lepidus had participated in the Sicilian campaign but later attempted to claim Sicily for himself. Octavian confronted Lepidus with his legions, and Lepidus's soldiers, recognizing which way the wind was blowing, defected to Octavian. Lepidus was forced into retirement and stripped of his triumviral powers, though he was allowed to retain the largely ceremonial position of pontifex maximus until his death in 13 BCE. The Second Triumvirate was now effectively reduced to Octavian and Antony.

But Octavian understood something Antony did not. Controlling Italy meant controlling Rome, and controlling Rome meant controlling the legitimacy that mattered for long-term power. Antony could rule the wealthy East, but Octavian held the symbolic and political heart of the Roman state.

### Antony and Cleopatra: The Love Story That Lost an Empire

While Octavian dealt with angry Italian landowners and restive veterans, Antony went east and met Cleopatra VII, queen of Egypt and the former lover of Julius Caesar.

The meeting was political theater. Ancient sources, particularly Plutarch, describe Cleopatra arriving at Tarsus in 41 BCE on a magnificent barge with purple sails, silver oars, and herself dressed as the goddess Venus. It is not known whether the meeting was this dramatic or if later historians embellished it. However, it is clear that Cleopatra needed Roman protection for her throne, and Antony needed Egypt's wealth to fund his eastern campaigns.

They also became lovers. The relationship was genuine. Ancient accounts suggest real affection between them, not just political convenience. Cleopatra was intelligent, educated, charismatic, and one of the few people who could match wits with Antony. Plutarch, who wrote over a century later, claims she spoke multiple languages, including Egyptian. She was politically skilled, having survived court intrigue and civil war to secure her throne. And she had resources, namely Egypt's grain and gold.

Antony and Cleopatra had three children together: twins Alexander Helios and Cleopatra Selene in 40 BCE and Ptolemy Philadelphus in 36 BCE. Antony divided his time between Alexandria and his military campaigns, spending winters in Egypt with Cleopatra and campaigning in the summer.

However, Antony's relationship with Cleopatra created political problems in Rome. Romans hated kings and queens. They particularly hated foreign queens who might influence Roman politics. Memories of Caesar's affair with Cleopatra (she had lived in Rome during Caesar's lifetime) fed fears that Antony was being seduced by Eastern luxury and abandoning Roman values.

Octavian exploited these fears brilliantly. He couldn't openly attack Antony—they were still technically allies, though the alliance was fraying—but he could attack Cleopatra. Octavian's propaganda machine portrayed Cleopatra as a dangerous foreign seductress who had enslaved Antony, turned him against Rome, and aimed to make herself queen of the Roman Empire. Ancient sources suggest that Octavian spread rumors that Antony was constantly drunk, had "gone native" and adopted Egyptian customs, and planned to move Rome's capital to Alexandria.

These charges had some basis in reality. Antony did spend significant time in Egypt. He did have children with Cleopatra. He participated in Egyptian ceremonies and adopted some Eastern customs. In 34 BCE, Antony held a ceremony in Alexandria known as the "Donations of Alexandria," during which he distributed eastern territories to Cleopatra and their children. He declared Cleopatra "Queen of Kings" and Caesarion—Cleopatra's son by Julius Caesar—"King of Kings." He gave Alexander Helios territories in the East, Cleopatra Selene territories in North Africa, and Ptolemy Philadelphus territories in Syria.

Romans were outraged. Antony was giving away Roman territories, or at least territories Rome claimed, to an Egyptian queen and her children. He was treating Caesarion as Caesar's legitimate heir, which challenged Octavian's position as Caesar's adopted son and heir. He was conducting himself like an Eastern monarch rather than a Roman magistrate.

Octavian seized the opportunity. He claimed Antony had abandoned Rome and Roman values. He broke into the Temple of the Vestal Virgins in Rome, where Roman wills were stored, and seized Antony's will—a sacrilegious act that showed Octavian's ruthlessness. Octavian claimed the will proved Antony wanted to be buried in Alexandria with Cleopatra rather than in Rome. He also supposedly wanted to make Caesarion Caesar's heir and planned to make Cleopatra queen of Rome. Whether the will actually said these things or whether Octavian fabricated parts of it is debated by modern scholars, but the political effect was devastating.

The Senate, dominated by Octavian's supporters, stripped Antony of his powers and declared war, not on Antony, but on Cleopatra. This was clever. Octavian avoided declaring civil war on a Roman citizen. Instead, Rome was defending itself against a foreign queen who threatened Roman independence. Antony was merely the unfortunate Roman general who had been seduced and corrupted by this dangerous foreign woman.

It was propaganda, but it was effective propaganda. By 32 BCE, Octavian had successfully painted the coming conflict not as a civil war between Romans but as a patriotic defense of Rome against foreign conquest.

### The Battle of Actium: The Shortest "Battle" That Changed History

In 31 BCE, the forces of Octavian and Antony finally met. Ancient sources provide varying estimates, but Antony and Cleopatra appear to have gathered substantial forces in Greece, perhaps around five hundred ships and seventy-five thousand infantry. Octavian commanded similar forces, led by his general Marcus Vipsanius Agrippa, one of the most competent military commanders in Roman history and Octavian's closest friend and ally.

The two fleets met near Actium on the western coast of Greece on September 2nd, 31 BCE. What happened next is one of the most debated events in Roman history because the ancient accounts contradict each other and are colored by pro-Octavian propaganda.

The traditional narrative, found in sources like Plutarch, says Antony's fleet was larger but became trapped in the Gulf of Actium by Agrippa's blockade. Antony's crews were sick, supplies were running low, and desertion was increasing. When battle came, Antony's fleet tried to break through the blockade. During the fighting, Cleopatra's squadron—perhaps sixty ships—suddenly hoisted sails and fled south toward Egypt. Antony, seeing Cleopatra flee, abandoned his fleet and followed her with a few ships. His fleet was left leaderless and surrendered or was destroyed. Antony's army surrendered shortly afterward.

The pro-Octavian interpretation was that Antony was so besotted with Cleopatra that he abandoned his army and fleet to follow his lover. This was the ultimate proof that he had been corrupted by foreign seduction and was unfit to lead the Romans.

Modern historians have questioned this narrative. Some suggest Actium was not a great naval battle but a strategic retreat that went wrong. Antony's position was untenable. Perhaps he planned to break out with his best ships, escape to Egypt, and regroup.

If so, the plan failed. Most of Antony's fleet did not break through, and his army surrendered. Antony and Cleopatra reached Egypt, but without an army or fleet, they were finished.

Octavian spent several months securing the eastern provinces and Antony's former territories. He moved slowly and deliberately, letting Antony's remaining support collapse. By the time Octavian reached Egypt in 30 BCE, Antony and Cleopatra's position was hopeless.

Ancient sources describe their final days with dramatic flair. Antony supposedly heard false rumors that Cleopatra was dead and stabbed himself, only to learn she was alive. He asked to be carried to her monument to die in her arms. Cleopatra, captured by Octavian's forces and held under guard, allegedly killed herself with an asp, a poisonous snake, rather than be paraded through Rome in Octavian's triumph. Modern scholars debate whether the snake story is true or a legend, but Cleopatra definitely died in Egypt. Octavian claimed Egypt as his personal property rather than a Roman province.

Octavian had Caesarion, Cleopatra's son by Julius Caesar, executed. Octavian could not allow a potential rival who claimed to be Caesar's biological son to survive. Cleopatra's other children were spared and raised in Rome by Octavian's sister Octavia, who had been married to Antony before he left her for Cleopatra.

The civil wars were over. Octavian stood alone. No armies opposed him. No rivals remained. The Roman world was his to reshape.

### The Principate: How to Become Emperor Without Calling Yourself King

Octavian returned to Rome in 29 BCE. He celebrated three triumphs for his victories. The Senate voted him honors. He was the undisputed master of the Roman state. However, he faced a crucial question: what to do with his power?

Octavian had learned from Caesar's mistakes. Caesar had accumulated power openly, accepted honors that suggested monarchy, and was assassinated by senators who claimed to be defending the Roman Republic. Octavian understood that Romans hated kings and loved the republic, or at least the idea of the republic. If Octavian wanted to rule without being assassinated, he needed to rule without appearing to be a king.

In 27 BCE, he appeared before the Senate and announced that he was restoring the republic. He resigned all his extraordinary powers and returned control of the provinces to the Senate. Octavian presented himself as a loyal citizen who had saved Rome from civil war and now wished to retire to private life, content that the republic was restored.

The Senate, dominated by Octavian's supporters and allies, reacted as Octavian knew it would. The senators begged him not to retire. They insisted Rome needed his leadership. They voted him honors and powers: the name "Augustus" (meaning "revered" or "majestic"), control of the most important provinces (those with significant military forces), supreme command of the army (*imperium*), and the authority of a tribune (including sacrosanctity and veto power).

This was the foundation of the Principate, the system of government that would last for centuries. On the surface, it looked as though the Roman Republic still existed. The Senate still met. Magistrates were still elected. Laws were still passed. But beneath the surface, Augustus controlled everything that mattered: the army, the wealthy provinces, and the grain supply that fed Rome.

Augustus called himself *princeps*, meaning "first citizen." He was not a king. Not a dictator. Just the first among equals in the Roman state. This was fiction, but it was carefully maintained fiction. Augustus was careful to respect the Senate, at least publicly. He consulted it on important matters. He allowed it to govern some provinces and treated senior senators with respect. He lived relatively modestly compared to Hellenistic monarchs, in a large but not palace-like house on Palatine Hill.

But Augustus's power was absolute. He controlled the provinces with legions. These provinces generated most of Rome's revenue and contained most of Rome's military force. The Senate controlled peaceful, urbanized provinces such as Greece and Asia Minor that had no legions. Augustus appointed the governors of his provinces directly. He could override the Senate when necessary. His word was effectively law.

Augustus also revolutionized the Roman administration. He created a professional civil service, using talented men from the equestrian class to administer finances, the grain supply, and imperial provinces. He reformed the army, reducing it to approximately 28 legions (around 150,000 men) of professional soldiers who served long-term enlistments and received land grants upon retirement. He established the Praetorian Guard, elite troops stationed in Italy, ostensibly to protect the emperor but also to enforce his power in Rome. He expanded the road network, postal system, and administrative infrastructure that made governing the empire possible.

He reformed taxation, creating regular census records and a systematic collection system. He established a treasury separate from the Senate's treasury to manage imperial funds. He founded colonies for veterans throughout the empire, spreading Roman culture and creating loyal communities. He beautified Rome with temples, forums, and public buildings, famously claiming that he "found Rome a city of brick and left it a city of marble."

Augustus also launched an ambitious program of social and moral reform, attempting to restore what he presented as traditional Roman values. In 18 and 17 BCE, he passed legislation to encourage marriage and childbearing among the upper classes. The Julian Laws penalized unmarried men and childless couples by restricting their inheritance rights while rewarding families with three or more children with legal privileges. He promoted marriage by making divorce more difficult and adultery a criminal offense; previously, it had been a private family matter.

These laws were deeply unpopular with the Roman elite, who resented state interference in private life. The laws were regularly evaded and eventually modified. Ironically, Augustus's own family provided the most scandalous violation. His daughter, Julia, was caught in an adultery scandal in 2 BCE. Augustus was forced by his own laws to exile his daughter to a barren island.

Augustus also revived the traditional Roman religion, which had been neglected during the civil wars. According to his own *Res Gestae*, a record of his achievements that he had inscribed throughout the empire, he rebuilt eighty-two temples in Rome. He revived ancient priesthoods and rituals that had fallen into disuse and promoted traditional festivals and ceremonies.

This religious revival served political purposes. By positioning himself as the restorer of tradition and piety, Augustus presented his rule as a return to Rome's glorious past rather than a revolutionary break with it. He also created a new religious dimension to imperial power: the cult of Augustus.

In the provinces, particularly the Greek East, ruler worship was traditional. Hellenistic kings had been worshiped as gods for centuries. Augustus carefully managed this practice. He discouraged worship of himself as a god in Italy during his lifetime, as that was too close to kingship for Roman sensibilities. However, he encouraged worship of Roma and the Divine Julius (the deified Caesar) alongside his *genius* (his divine spirit or guardian). In the Eastern provinces, he allowed temples to be built for "Rome and Augustus," positioning himself as Rome's representative rather than claiming personal divinity.

After his death, the Senate declared him divine—*Divus Augustus*—and established an official cult with priests and temples. His successors would follow this pattern. Emperors were mortal men during their lifetime but could be declared gods after death, if the Senate approved. This helped legitimize the emperor's power.

Augustus also addressed the crucial problem of succession. He had no sons, only a daughter, Julia. Roman law and custom had no clear way for transferring power because, officially, Rome was still a republic and Augustus was just another magistrate. But unofficially, Augustus needed to build a dynasty.

His succession planning became a decades-long tragedy of premature deaths and dashed hopes. Augustus first groomed his nephew Marcellus (the son of his sister Octavia) by marrying him to Julia in 25 BCE, when Marcellus was about seventeen, and Julia was fourteen. However, Marcellus died of illness in 23 BCE at age nineteen or twenty. Augustus then married Julia to his closest friend and general, Marcus Agrippa, in 21 BCE. Agrippa was much older than Julia, but the match was political. Julia and Agrippa had five children, including two sons, Gaius and Lucius Caesar.

Augustus adopted Gaius and Lucius as his own sons in 17 BCE, making them his heirs. He advanced them rapidly through political honors and military commands, grooming them to succeed him. Roman hopes for a smooth succession centered on these young princes. But tragedy struck again. Lucius died in 2 CE at age nineteen, possibly of illness. Gaius died in 4 CE at age twenty-three from wounds received while fighting in Armenia.

With both designated heirs dead, Augustus turned to his stepson, Tiberius. Tiberius was from Livia's first marriage to Tiberius Claudius Nero. He was capable, experienced, and had proven himself in military campaigns in Pannonia and Germany. But Augustus had previously treated him as second-tier; Tiberius was a useful commander but not heir material. In 12 BCE, Augustus forced Tiberius to divorce his beloved wife, Vipsania (Agrippa's daughter from his first marriage), to marry Julia, Augustus's daughter and Agrippa's widow. This was a loveless political marriage. Ancient sources suggest Julia and Tiberius loathed each other.

Julia's behavior became increasingly scandalous. Ancient sources, particularly Suetonius, describe her conducting affairs openly, even reportedly using the Forum itself. Whether the stories were true or exaggerated by hostile sources, Julia's behavior violated Augustus's own moral legislation. In 2 BCE, Augustus was forced to acknowledge his daughter's adultery. He exiled Julia to the island of Pandateria, forbade her wine and luxuries, and refused to see her again. Several of her alleged lovers were executed or exiled.

The scandal was devastating to Augustus and politically damaging to his image as a moral reformer. But it also removed complications from the succession process. With Julia exiled and disgraced, Tiberius was clearly Augustus's heir.

Augustus adopted Tiberius in 4 CE, along with his last surviving grandson, Agrippa Postumus (Julia's youngest son with Agrippa). Agrippa Postumus proved difficult; ancient sources describe him as coarse and possibly mentally unstable. Augustus eventually exiled him in 7 CE. When Augustus died in 14 CE, Agrippa Postumus was quietly executed, removing any potential rival to Tiberius. Some ancient sources and modern scholars have speculated about Livia's role in the convenient deaths and exiles of Augustus's preferred heirs, though evidence for such involvement remains circumstantial and debated.

Tiberius succeeded Augustus smoothly despite his tragic path to power. The Principate would continue. Augustus had established a system flexible enough to survive succession crises and transfer power across generations.

### The Pax Romana: What Peace Meant in an Empire Built on Conquest

One of Augustus's greatest achievements–and most effective propaganda claims–was bringing peace after a century of civil wars. The *Pax Romana* (Roman Peace) became synonymous with Augustus's reign. But what did this "peace" actually mean?

For Romans in Italy, peace was real. No armies marched through Italian cities. No proscriptions terrorized the elite. No rival warlords fought for supremacy. Trade flourished. Roads were safe. The grain supply was secure. After generations of civil war, Italians experienced genuine stability. Augustus had ended the cycle of Roman killing Roman that had consumed the republic.

However, the Pax Romana was not universal peace. Rome's borders expanded under Augustus through continuous military campaigns. In the north, Roman armies conquered the Alpine regions, pushing Rome's frontier to the Danube River. Generals such as Tiberius and Drusus (Augustus's stepsons) campaigned for years in Pannonia, Raetia, and Germania, subduing tribes and establishing Roman control. These were not defensive wars; they were wars of conquest aimed at expanding Roman territory and glorifying Augustus through military victories.

The conquest of Germania proved particularly costly. From 12 to 9 BCE, Drusus campaigned successfully east of the Rhine, penetrating deep into Germanic territory. After Drusus died from injuries in 9 BCE, other commanders continued the expansion. By 9 CE, the Romans believed that Germania up to the Elbe River had been pacified and could be organized as a Roman province.

Then disaster struck. In 9 CE, the Germanic chieftain Arminius, who had served in Roman auxiliaries and held Roman citizenship, turned against Rome. He ambushed three Roman legions under the command of Publius Quinctilius Varus in the Teutoburg Forest. Over three days of fighting in terrible terrain during a rainstorm, Germanic warriors destroyed the legions almost completely. Ancient sources suggest perhaps fifteen thousand to twenty thousand Roman soldiers died. Varus committed suicide.

When Augustus received news of the disaster, he was devastated. For months afterward, he allegedly banged his head against doors, crying, "Quinctili Vare, legiones redde!"—"Quintilius Varus, give me back my legions!" The defeat traumatized Augustus in his final years. Rome never again seriously attempted to conquer Germania beyond the Rhine. The disaster at the Teutoburg Forest essentially fixed Rome's northern frontier for centuries.

In the East, Augustus pursued a different strategy. Rather than costly conquests, he established client kingdoms. These were nominally independent states ruled by friendly kings who accepted Roman supremacy. Judea, Armenia, and other eastern territories were governed through this system, giving Rome control without the expense of direct administration. When client kings proved unreliable, Rome intervened or annexed territories, but it preferred indirect rule.

In Egypt, Augustus took a unique approach. He treated Egypt as his personal property rather than a normal Roman province. Senators were forbidden from entering Egypt without Augustus's permission. He appointed equestrians rather than senators to govern Egypt. Egypt's enormous wealth belonged to Augustus personally, not the Roman state, which gave Augustus financial independence from the Senate and ensured that no rival could seize Egypt's resources.

For conquered peoples, the Pax Romana meant enforced peace. Roman legions stationed throughout the provinces maintained order. Revolts were crushed brutally. Tribes that resisted were enslaved or massacred. Roman governors extracted taxes, requisitioned supplies, and demanded military conscription from subject peoples. The benefits of Roman rule, including roads, aqueducts, legal systems, and urban development, came with costs like taxation, conscription, loss of independence, and Roman cultural dominance.

However, for many provincials, Roman rule offered advantages compared to previous alternatives. Roman law was more predictable than that of arbitrary local rulers. Roman citizenship brought legal protections and economic opportunities. Roman military presence suppressed banditry and tribal warfare. Roman infrastructure connected provinces to larger trade networks. Cities prospered under Roman administration. The Romanization of the provinces would ultimately create a unified Mediterranean civilization that lasted for centuries.

## The Julio-Claudians: When "Mad" Emperors Proved the System Worked

Augustus died in 14 CE. The question everyone had was whether the system could survive without him. The next hundred years would answer that question. The Julio-Claudian dynasty—five emperors connected by blood or adoption to Julius Caesar and Augustus—would include competent administrators, cautious rulers, and, according to ancient sources, at least two emperors who were genuinely insane. Yet the empire not only survived; it also prospered. This proved that Augustus had built something more durable than personal rule. He had created an imperial system.

### Tiberius (r. 14–37 CE): The Reluctant Emperor

Tiberius succeeded Augustus at age fifty-five after a long military career. Ancient sources, particularly Tacitus and Suetonius, paint Tiberius as gloomy, suspicious, and increasingly tyrannical. But the historical reality was more complex. Tiberius was a capable administrator who upheld Augustus's policies, maintained peace in the provinces, and managed finances responsibly. The treasury was fuller when he died than when he took power, which is still a rare achievement for any ruler.

Tiberius's problem was political theater. Augustus had been a master performer, playing the modest first citizen while wielding absolute power. Tiberius was competent but awkward. He was uncomfortable with the

Senate's flattery and ill-suited to the social aspects of ruling. He reportedly hated giving games and public spectacles that the Romans expected. His relationship with the Senate was tense. He expected senators to debate and advise, but they had learned under Augustus to defer to imperial wishes.

The most notorious aspect of Tiberius's reign was the rise of Sejanus, the Praetorian prefect who became Tiberius's chief minister. Ancient sources accuse Sejanus of manipulating Tiberius, conducting treason trials to eliminate rivals, and plotting to seize power. Whether Sejanus was truly a villain or Tacitus exaggerated his role is debated. What is clear is that when Tiberius finally turned against Sejanus in 31 CE, he had him executed along with his supporters, family members, and even his children.

In 26 CE, Tiberius retired to Capri, an island off southern Italy. He never returned to Rome. Instead, he governed the empire through correspondence for the last eleven years of his reign. While Rome remained administratively stable during this period, ancient sources describe increasing paranoia and reliance on informers, leading to heightened purges and treason trials. These sources also include scandalous stories. Tacitus and Suetonius describe debauched parties and perverse acts. Modern historians note that regardless of Tiberius's personal behavior or increasing isolation, the empire's administration continued to function, though whether this represents effective governance or was merely momentum from Augustus's reign remains debated.

### Caligula (r. 37–41 CE): Four Years of Increasing Madness

When Tiberius died in 37 CE, the Romans rejoiced. His successor was Gaius Caesar, known as Caligula ("Little Boots," a nickname from his childhood in military camps). Caligula was the son of Germanicus, a beloved general, and a great-grandson of Augustus. Romans had high hopes.

Those hopes lasted about seven months. According to ancient sources, Caligula began his reign with sensible policies, moderate behavior, and popularity. Then he fell seriously ill. When he recovered, ancient historians claim he was a different person. He was paranoid, cruel, and possibly insane.

What followed, if ancient sources are to be believed, was one of the strangest reigns in Roman history. Caligula declared himself a living god and built temples for his own worship. He reportedly had conversations with statues of Jupiter. He planned to make his horse Incitatus a consul, though this might have been a mockery of the Senate rather than genuine madness. He executed senators and equestrians on a whim. Ancient sources claim he slept with his sisters, particularly Drusilla. When Drusilla died in 38 CE, he forced the Senate to declare her a goddess. He spent enormous sums on bizarre projects, exhausting Tiberius's carefully managed treasury. Caligula humiliated the Senate by forcing senators to run alongside his chariot. He led a military "campaign" to Germany and Gaul that achieved nothing, then had his troops collect seashells from the beach as "spoils of conquering the Ocean."

Modern historians debate how much of this is true. Ancient sources such as Suetonius and Cassius Dio wrote decades later from the perspective of the senatorial class–the very people Caligula oppressed. The sources contradict each other on specific events. Many of Caligula's alleged acts of "madness" are now seen as deliberate political theater or calculated insults to the Senate that were later recast as insanity. Some actions might have been provocations meant to test the limits of imperial power and humiliate senators who had collaborated in his family's destruction under Tiberius.

But several facts are clear. Caligula became increasingly autocratic, rejecting Augustus's fiction of being merely "first citizen." He emphasized his absolute power and divine status. He executed senators he suspected of disloyalty. He depleted the treasury. After less than four years as emperor, the Praetorian Guard assassinated him in 41 CE, becoming the first Roman emperor murdered by his own troops.

### Claudius (r. 41–54 CE): The Unlikely Emperor Who Conquered Britain

After Caligula's assassination, the Praetorian Guard found Claudius hiding behind a curtain in the palace. Claudius was Caligula's uncle. He was a fifty-year-old man with physical disabilities. Ancient sources describe a limp, a stutter, and involuntary movements that Romans interpreted as signs of stupidity. The imperial family had kept him out of politics, considering him an embarrassment.

The Praetorians decided to make him emperor anyway, possibly because he was the only adult male Julian left alive, and they wanted someone controllable. They were wrong about the controllable part.

Claudius proved to be an excellent administrator. He was educated; he had written histories and studied under scholars during his years of political exclusion. He expanded the imperial bureaucracy, using freedmen (former slaves) as ministers to manage finances, correspondence, and petitions. This professionalized the imperial administration but offended senatorial sensibilities. Freed slaves wielding power over senators was humiliating to the aristocracy.

Claudius's greatest achievement was the conquest of Britain. In 43 CE, he launched a full-scale invasion with four legions. Previous Roman expeditions to Britain, such as Julius Caesar's raids, had achieved little. Claudius's invasion was a systematic conquest. Roman forces defeated British tribes, captured the stronghold of Camulodunum (modern Colchester), and established Roman control over southern Britain. Claudius personally visited Britain for sixteen days to accept the surrender of British chiefs.

Claudius also extended Roman citizenship more liberally, incorporated Gallic nobles into the Senate, and built infrastructure, including new harbors and aqueducts. Ancient sources credit him with generally sound governance, though they also portray him as being dominated by his wives and freedmen.

His personal life was messier. Claudius's fourth wife was his niece Agrippina the Younger (daughter of Germanicus and sister of Caligula). Agrippina was described as ambitious and ruthless. She persuaded Claudius to adopt her son Nero and make him heir instead of Claudius's own son, Britannicus. In 54 CE, Claudius died; ancient sources claim Agrippina poisoned him with mushrooms. Whether this is true or Claudius died naturally is unknown, but Agrippina's son Nero became emperor at age sixteen.

### Nero (r. 54–68 CE): The Artist Emperor Who Burned Rome (Allegedly)

Nero was guided by capable advisors, the philosopher Seneca and the Praetorian Prefect Burrus. For the first five years, Nero's government was competent. Ancient sources call this period the *Quinquennium Neronis*—Nero's five good years.

But Nero wanted to be an artist, not an administrator. He was passionate about music, poetry, theater, and chariot racing. He wanted to perform publicly, which Romans considered inappropriate for someone of his status. Entertainment was for professionals and slaves, not emperors. Nero did not care. He performed in theaters, sang at public events, and raced chariots. To elite Romans, this was humiliating. To common people, Nero was popular. He sponsored games and entertainment and seemed more accessible than distant, aristocratic emperors.

Nero's reign grew darker as he consolidated power. In 59 CE, he arranged his mother's murder. In 62 CE, Burrus died, and Seneca retired, removing stabilizing influences. Nero married Poppaea Sabina after divorcing his first wife, Octavia (Claudius's daughter), whom he then had executed on false adultery charges.

Then, in 64 CE, came the Great Fire of Rome. The fire burned for six days, destroying large portions of the city. Romans needed someone to blame. Ancient sources written by senatorial historians hostile to Nero claim he started the fire, that he wanted to clear space for a massive palace complex called the Domus Aurea ("Golden House"). Whether Nero was actually responsible is unknown and heavily debated by modern scholars. What is documented is that Nero accused Christians—then a small, unpopular sect—of arson to deflect blame. The historian Tacitus, writing about fifty years later, describes brutal persecutions. Christians were burned alive as torches, torn apart by dogs, and crucified. The extent of these persecutions is debated, but this episode marks the first major Roman persecution of Christians.

Nero built his Golden House on cleared land in central Rome. It was a massive palace complex with artificial lakes, pavilions, and, supposedly, a hundred-foot statue of Nero as the sun god. The extravagance shocked Romans.

In 65 CE, senators and officers plotted to assassinate Nero (known as the Pisonian conspiracy). The plot was discovered. Nero executed dozens of conspirators and forced many prominent Romans to commit suicide, including Seneca. This reign of terror destroyed what remained of Nero's support among the elite.

By 68 CE, provincial governors were in revolt. The governor of Hispania, Galba, marched on Rome with his legions. The Praetorian Guard defected to Galba. The Senate declared Nero an enemy of the state. Nero fled Rome and committed suicide, allegedly saying, "What an artist dies in me!" as he prepared to kill himself. Nero's death ended the Julio-Claudian dynasty.

The dynasty's collapse triggered a brief civil war known as the Year of the Four Emperors. Within a year, Vespasian, a capable general from a non-aristocratic family, established a new dynasty and restored order. The empire endured.

A bust of Vespasian.[15]

# Chapter 7: Bread, Circuses, and Bathhouses: What It Was Actually Like to Live in the Roman Empire

History books love emperors, generals, and battles. But most Romans never commanded an army, never saw the emperor, and spent their lives working, eating, gossiping, and trying to survive in crowded cities or on rural farms. So, what was life actually like for regular people in the Roman Empire?

Let's find out by following a typical day for someone living in Rome during the empire's peak—say, around 150 CE, under Emperor Antoninus Pius. Rome had about a million residents, making it the largest city in the ancient world. Most people were not wealthy senators or merchants. They were the urban poor and working class, living in apartment buildings and scraping by on whatever work they could find.

### A Day in the Life: Living in a Roman Insula

You wake up in your *insula*, a multistory apartment building, the ancient Roman equivalent of a modern apartment complex. However, this is nothing like a nice modern apartment.

Your apartment is on the fifth floor. That's not ideal. The higher you live, the cheaper the rent, but it was also more dangerous. *Insulae* in Rome were thrown up quickly and cheaply, often exceeding height limits. Your building sways in strong winds. The wooden floors creak ominously.

You have heard stories of entire buildings collapsing, killing everyone inside. It happens often enough that you try not to think about it.

Your apartment is one room; it is maybe two hundred to three hundred square feet for an entire family. There is no kitchen, no bathroom, and no running water. There is definitely no plumbing. The walls are thin wood and plaster, so you can hear everything your neighbors do. The ceiling is low. The single window faces a narrow alley, so not much light gets in. During the summer, it is unbearably hot. During winter, it is freezing, and you huddle around a small brazier that fills the room with smoke since there is no chimney.

You sleep on a simple wooden bed frame with a straw mattress. Your furniture consists of a small table, a couple of stools, and maybe a chest for storing clothes and valuables. That is it. You are fortunate to have that much. Many poorer Romans sleep on the floor.

The first thing you notice when you wake up is the noise. Rome never sleeps. All night, you have been hearing wagons rumbling through the streets—delivery carts that are only allowed in the city after dark to reduce daytime congestion. You have heard people shouting, singing, and fighting. You have heard your neighbors arguing, making love, and dealing with crying babies. The building itself creaks and groans. And now, as dawn approaches, the noise increases as the city wakes.

You need to urinate. This is a problem. There is no toilet in your apartment. You have a chamber pot, which you empty into a large jar. When the jar is full, you are supposed to carry it down five flights of stairs and dump it into the public sewer. But that is annoying, and the stairs are dark and dangerous. So, like many Romans, you sometimes just throw it out the window into the street. There are laws against this—people have been fined when falling waste injures pedestrians—but it happens often enough that walking Rome's streets at night is genuinely dangerous.

There is no water in your apartment either. On the fifth floor, you must carry water up from the ground floor or from a public fountain in the street. Lower floors of some insulae have access to cisterns or basic plumbing, but you are too high up. Every day, someone in your family makes multiple trips up and down five flights of stairs carrying heavy water containers. This is exhausting and time-consuming. Wealthy Romans have running water piped directly to their houses. You do not.

For breakfast, you eat bread soaked in watered wine or water, perhaps with some chickpeas or lentils if you have them. Bread is the staple of the Roman diet. Legumes, like lentils, chickpeas, and beans, provide the primary protein for the urban poor. The government provides a free grain dole (*annona*) to eligible Roman citizens. About 200,000 people receive free grain monthly, though eligibility requirements mean that not all poor Romans qualify. This is not charity; it is politics. Emperors learned long ago that keeping the urban poor fed prevents riots. The term "bread and circuses" refers to giving the masses food and entertainment so that they will stay peaceful.

If you are not eligible for the grain dole, you must buy your food. Bread from a bakery costs a few *asses* (small bronze coins). You might also buy olives, garlic, onions, or legumes from a street vendor or the market. If you are doing well, perhaps you will buy some cheese. Meat is expensive and rare. You may eat it a few times a month, usually pork or chicken.

You do not cook at home because there is no kitchen and because open flames in wooden buildings are disasters waiting to happen. Rome experiences fires frequently. Small fires occur regularly, and major conflagrations such as the Great Fire of 64 CE under Nero, which destroyed huge portions of the city, demonstrate the catastrophic potential. Your landlord has forbidden cooking fires in the apartments, though some people do it anyway and hope they do not burn the building down.

So, you eat food from street vendors or from taverns called *popinae*. These are everywhere in Rome (archaeological evidence suggests there were thousands of food establishments throughout the city). You can buy hot porridge, stews, grilled meats, bread, vegetables, and wine. It is essentially Roman fast food. It is not fancy, but it is cheap and convenient.

You head out for work. Perhaps you work at the docks unloading ships, at a construction site hauling materials, or in a warehouse organizing goods. You are paid daily, usually a few sesterces (larger bronze coins). This is enough to cover food, rent, and little else. You have no job security. If you are injured or sick and cannot work, you do not get paid. If there is no work available today, you do not eat today.

Or perhaps you are a shopkeeper, a craftsman, or part of a trade guild. If so, you are doing somewhat better. You have a more stable income and a higher social status. But you still live in an insula and still deal with the same noise, dirt, and fire risks. Even middle-class Romans lived in apartments, not houses. Only the wealthy owned private *domus*, houses with courtyards, multiple rooms, gardens, and private water supplies.

Rome's streets are crowded, noisy, and honestly kind of disgusting. The streets are narrow; many are only ten to fifteen feet wide. Buildings loom on both sides, blocking out the sun. The streets are paved with stone, which helps, but they are covered in filth. There is animal dung from horses, donkeys, and dogs. There is human waste thrown from windows. There is rotting garbage and puddles of unidentifiable liquids. You walk carefully, watching where you step.

The streets are packed with people: slaves running errands, merchants hawking goods, beggars asking for coins, prostitutes soliciting customers, performers entertaining crowds, and pickpockets looking for marks. Street vendors sell everything, from bread, fruit, vegetables, and wine to cooked food, cheap goods, and trinkets. The noise is overwhelming. People are shouting, haggling, arguing, and laughing. Animals bleat and bray. Wagons squeak, and hammers pound in workshops.

Rome is a sensory overload. It smells of smoke, human and animal waste, rotting garbage, perfumes and incense from shops and temples, food cooking, and leather tanning. It is loud and crowded beyond anything most modern cities experience. And it is exciting, vibrant, and alive in a way that makes rural life seem boring.

After a morning of work, you are hungry and tired. It is midday, so it is time for the most important part of a Roman's day: the baths.

### The Baths: More Than Just Washing–The Social Hub of the Empire

If you want to understand Roman culture, you need to understand the baths. Bathing was not just about getting clean. It was the social center of Roman life. It was where people relaxed, exercised, gossiped, conducted business, and spent hours every afternoon.

Rome had hundreds of baths. There were small private baths run by individuals or companies that charged a small entry fee, perhaps a *quadrans*, the smallest coin, about a quarter of an *as*. Then there were the massive imperial baths. These were gigantic complexes built by emperors and opened to the public for either free or for a small fee. The Baths of Trajan, completed in 109 CE, and the older Baths of Agrippa could accommodate hundreds or even thousands of bathers. These were more than just bathhouses; they were also massive recreational complexes with gardens, libraries, meeting rooms, exercise areas, and more.

You would pay your entrance fee (or enter for free if it is a public day) and check your clothes in the changing room. Theft was common, so attendants watched your clothes, though you might still bribe an attendant or have a slave guard your possessions. Romans bathed naked, which was not considered immodest but normal and practical.

The bathing process followed a specific routine. You started in the *palaestra,* an exercise courtyard. Here, people engaged in various physical activities like wrestling, ball games, weightlifting, and running. Romans valued physical fitness and believed exercise was essential to health. You might spend thirty minutes to an hour working up a good sweat.

Then you moved inside to begin bathing. First was the *tepidarium,* a warm room that helped your body adjust to the heat. This was like a warm-up, a transitional space between the cool outside and the hot baths. You might spend ten to fifteen minutes here, chatting with friends and letting your body acclimate.

Next came the *caldarium,* the hot room. This was where you really start to sweat. The room was heated by a hypocaust, an underfloor heating system in which hot air from furnaces circulated beneath the floor and through spaces in the walls. The floor was literally hot enough that Romans wore wooden sandals to avoid burning their feet. There was a hot-water pool where they could soak. After fifteen to twenty minutes, you would be thoroughly heated and sweating.

Now came the actual cleaning. Romans did not use soap; they used olive oil. You or a slave rubbed your body with oil, then scraped it off with a curved metal tool called a *strigil.* The oil pulled the dirt and dead skin from your body. It was surprisingly effective.

Then you moved to the *frigidarium,* the cold room. This had a cold-water pool. It was often unheated and quite bracing. After being overheated in the caldarium, plunging into cold water was shocking but invigorating. Romans believed the contrast in temperature was healthy. You might spend only a few minutes here before exiting.

Finally, you dried off, got dressed, and perhaps relaxed in one of the bath's gardens or sitting rooms.

However, the bathing itself was almost secondary to the social experience. The baths were where Romans of all classes mingled. A poor laborer might bathe next to a wealthy merchant. Slaves attended their masters. Baths typically had separate hours or separate facilities for men and women, though mixed bathing occurred in some places, often scandalizing more conservative Romans.

People conducted business at the baths. Lawyers met clients. Merchants negotiated deals. Politicians canvassed for support. The baths were where Romans networked, exchanged information, and built relationships. There is no modern equivalent. Imagine if the gym, the coffee shop, the spa, the library, and the town square all existed in one place, and everyone in the city went there every afternoon.

You also heard all the city's gossip at the baths: who was sleeping with whom, which senator was in political trouble, what the emperor had done recently, which businesses were thriving or failing, which neighborhoods were dangerous, and what new laws were being proposed. Information flowed through the baths like water through the pools.

The baths had other amenities too. There were often libraries where educated Romans could read. There were massage rooms where you could pay for a rubdown. There were snack bars where you could buy food and wine. There were hair removal services, as Romans valued hairless bodies and used various painful methods to achieve this. There were vendors selling oils, perfumes, and grooming supplies.

You might spend two to four hours at the baths. This was not considered wasteful or lazy. This was normal. In a society without television, the internet, or most forms of modern entertainment, the baths were the primary recreational activity for millions of Romans throughout the empire.

After the baths, you might head to dinner, or you might decide to do what hundreds of thousands of Romans did several times a year: attend the games.

## The Colosseum: The Logistics of Blood Sport and Why Romans Loved It

The Colosseum is Rome's most famous building. Completed in 80 CE under Emperor Titus, it could hold between fifty thousand and eighty thousand spectators. It is an engineering marvel. It is 159 feet tall, 620 feet long, built from travertine stone and concrete, and has a complex system of corridors, staircases, trapdoors, and underground chambers.

**The Colosseum.**[16]

But let's talk about what happened inside: the games.

Roman games included several types of spectacles. There were theatrical performances, athletic competitions, and public executions. But what Romans really loved were gladiatorial combat and animal hunts.

Let's say you are attending the games on a festival day. Entry is free; emperors sponsor the games as a gift to the Roman people. You arrive early because getting a good seat requires showing up hours before the games begin. Your seating is determined by social class. Senators sit in the front rows, close to the action. Equestrians sit behind them. Regular citizens sit in the middle tiers. Women, slaves, and the poorest Romans sit in the highest sections, far from the arena floor. Your social status is literally visible in where you sit.

The seating system is actually quite sophisticated. Each entrance is numbered, and your section is marked. You enter through one of the eighty ground-level arches, climb stairs to your level, and find your seat. The architects designed it so efficiently that the entire Colosseum could be evacuated in minutes if necessary. Modern stadiums still use similar principles.

The games typically begin in the morning with animal hunts (*venationes*). The arena floor is set up to resemble a landscape with artificial trees, rocks, and painted backdrops. Then the animals are released. You might see lions, bears, elephants, leopards, crocodiles, ostriches, bulls, or other exotic creatures. Professional hunters called *venatores* fight and kill the animals while the crowd cheers.

These animal hunts were spectacular and expensive. Ancient sources claim that nine thousand animals were killed during the Colosseum's inaugural games over one hundred days. Modern historians view this figure as a likely exaggeration, though the actual scale was still enormous. Animals were imported from Africa, Asia, and throughout the empire. Lions, elephants, and other exotic beasts were costly and difficult to transport. The logistics of moving large numbers of animals to Rome and keeping them alive in underground holding facilities beneath the Colosseum would have been a massive undertaking.

Modern people often find these animal hunts disturbing; killing animals for entertainment seems cruel and wasteful. Romans saw it differently. Wild animals represented untamed nature, chaos, and danger. Killing them demonstrated Roman power over nature and the empire's wild fringes.

At midday, there is a break for executions. Condemned criminals are brought into the arena and killed in various ways. Some are beheaded or crucified. Others are killed by animals, thrown to lions or bears, or tied to stakes while wild animals tear them apart. Sometimes the executions are staged as reenactments of myths. For instance, a criminal may be dressed as Icarus and dropped from a height, someone dressed as Orpheus may be torn apart by bears, or a criminal playing Hercules may be burned alive on a pyre.

This is the part of the games that is hardest for modern people to understand. Romans watched human beings as they were tortured and killed while treating it as entertainment. Romans believed criminals deserved harsh punishment. The people being executed had been convicted of serious crimes like murder, treason, armed robbery, and arson. In Roman thinking, they forfeited their humanity through their crimes. Making their deaths public and dramatic served as deterrence and retribution. It was also a display of the emperor's power to punish lawbreakers.

The main event would come in the afternoon: gladiatorial combat.

Gladiators came from various backgrounds. Many were enslaved prisoners of war or condemned criminals forced to fight. However, a significant number were free volunteers who signed contracts to become gladiators for a period of years. Why would free men volunteer for such a dangerous profession? They did it for money and fame.

Successful gladiators could become wealthy. They received prize money for victories, gifts from wealthy patrons, and the benefits of celebrity status. Famous gladiators' images appeared on oil lamps, pottery, and graffiti throughout the empire, not through commercial contracts like modern athlete endorsements but because fans wanted to display their favorite fighters. The most famous gladiators were celebrities comparable to modern athletes or movie stars. Free men might volunteer because they were poor and desperate, seeking glory, or simply because they enjoyed combat.

A mosaic of gladiators in combat.[17]

Gladiators trained in specialized schools (*ludi*) run by managers (*lanistae*). They trained in different fighting styles, each with distinctive weapons and armor. A *murmillo* wore a helmet with a fish crest and carried a short sword and a large rectangular shield. A *retiarius* had no helmet, carried a net and trident, and relied on speed and agility. A *thraex* used a small round shield and a curved sword. A *hoplomachus* was heavily armored, wielding a spear and a small shield.

Gladiatorial combat was more complex than "fight to the death." Matches were usually between gladiators of different styles, like a *murmillo* versus a *retiarius*, for example. The contrasting styles created interesting tactical matchups. The fights were real, dangerous, and sometimes fatal.

When you watch the gladiatorial match on the festival day, you see skilled fighters using real weapons in genuine combat. Blood is spilled. Injuries occur. But the goal is not always to kill. The goal is to win by forcing your opponent to surrender or by incapacitating them. If a gladiator is wounded or outmatched, he can appeal to the crowd for mercy by raising a finger.

Then comes the famous moment. The crowd and the sponsor of the games—often the emperor, if present—decide the loser's fate. The crowd expresses its opinion with gestures (though today we are not actually sure whether a thumbs-up meant life or death in Roman times; the sources are ambiguous). The sponsor makes the final decision, deciding the loser should live.

If the loser fought well, showed bravery, and pleased the crowd, he was usually spared. Killing gladiators was expensive. Gladiators required significant investment in training, feeding, and housing. Sponsors did not want to waste money killing gladiators unnecessarily. Most gladiators survived their fights. Studies of gladiator graves suggest mortality rates of around 10 to 20 percent per bout; the fights were still dangerous, but they did not lead to the guaranteed death sentence many imagine.

If the sponsor signaled for death, the winner delivered a killing blow. The loser was expected to accept death bravely without resistance or pleading—that was part of the gladiatorial code. Arena attendants dressed as Charon, the ferryman of the dead, would come out, confirm death by striking the body with a hammer, and drag the corpse away through the "Gate of Death." Fresh sand was spread over the blood, and the next match began.

Why did the Romans love this? Well, it was undeniably exciting. There was real danger, real skill, and unpredictable outcomes. It was a display of Roman virtues, including courage, discipline, skill in arms, and acceptance of fate. Gladiators who fought bravely embodied the Roman ideal of *virtus*—manly courage and excellence. Even though gladiators were legally *infames* (disgraced people), they were admired for their fighting ability.

The games also reinforced Roman identity and values. They displayed Roman power and wealth; only Rome could afford such spectacular entertainment. They demonstrated Roman control over life and death. They reminded Romans of their military heritage. Gladiatorial combat actually originated as funeral rites honoring dead warriors. And they provided a release for aggression and bloodlust in a controlled, legal setting.

For you, sitting in the stands, it is an afternoon of entertainment unlike anything else in the ancient world. You cheer for your favorite gladiators, boo the ones you dislike, eat snacks bought from vendors, chat with fellow spectators, and feel part of something larger. You are participating in a shared cultural experience with tens of thousands of other Romans. For a few hours, social hierarchies matter less. Rich and poor cheer together. You are all Romans, enjoying the gifts of the emperor, celebrating Roman culture, and bonding through shared bloodlust.

By late afternoon, the games end. You file out through the efficient exit system, return to your daily life, and look forward to the next games. If you are lucky, there will be another spectacle in a few weeks. And there is always tomorrow, when you can return to the baths and relive the day's excitement with fellow Romans.

But before we leave the subject of Roman daily life, we need to address the foundations that made it all possible: religion.

### Roman Religion: Why You're Praying to a Hundred Different Gods

Roman religion was everywhere in daily life, but it worked completely differently from modern religions.

Romans did not care so much what a person believed. They cared more about what a person did. There was no sacred text to study. No unified theology to debate. No creed to recite. What mattered was performing the correct rituals at the correct times. Sacrifice to the gods properly, and they would be favorable. Neglect the rituals, and the gods grew angry. And when the gods were angry, bad things happened to everyone.

Romans thought of religion as a kind of contract. You gave offerings to the gods, and the gods gave you benefits. This principle was called *do ut des*—"I give so that you may give." You sacrificed a sheep to Mars before battle. Mars got the sheep, and you expected a victory. If you lost, perhaps you had not sacrificed enough. Perhaps you had performed the ritual incorrectly. Perhaps you had offended Mars somehow.

Roman religion was also communal, not personal. It was not about an individual relationship with the divine or personal salvation. It was about maintaining the *pax deorum*—the peace with the gods that kept Rome prosperous. Religious rituals were public civic events. Priests were government officials. Temples were state institutions. Religion was a patriotic duty.

The Roman pantheon was crowded. At the top sat the Capitoline Triad: Jupiter (king of the gods), Juno (his wife, goddess of marriage), and Minerva (goddess of wisdom and war). Romans borrowed these gods from the Greeks. Jupiter was essentially Zeus under a Roman name, Juno was Hera, and Minerva was Athena.

There were dozens more gods: Mars for war, Venus for love, Apollo for prophecy and healing, Diana for hunting, Neptune for the sea, Mercury for commerce, Ceres for agriculture, and Bacchus for wine and intoxication. There were also countless minor deities and spirits. Every home had household guardians—Lares and Penates—who protected the family. Every river, grove, and crossroads had its own spirit.

Still, the Roman religion was remarkably tolerant. When the Romans conquered new territories, they did not suppress local religions. They absorbed them. The Germanic god Wotan became associated with Mercury. The Celtic goddess Sulis in Britain became Sulis Minerva. The Egyptian Isis and the Persian Mithras became popular in Rome. One more god was no problem—unless that religion threatened the social order.

The Romans persecuted Christians and Jews. It was not about worshiping an additional god; the Romans were comfortable with that. The problem was that Christians and Jews refused to participate in civic rituals and imperial cult worship. To Romans, that refusal was unpatriotic and dangerous.

This led to the imperial cult: the worship of emperors.

After Augustus died, the Senate declared him a god. Temples were built to worship *Divus Augustus*. This was not metaphorical. Romans believed Augustus had become divine after death. Later emperors could also be deified if the Senate judged them worthy.

The imperial cult went beyond worshiping dead emperors. Throughout the empire, especially in the eastern provinces where ruler worship had long been traditional, people built temples to the living emperor's *genius* (guardian spirit) or to Roma, the personification of

Rome, together with the emperor. The imperial cult was more prominent and elaborate in the Greek-speaking East than in Rome itself. Making offerings at these temples and swearing oaths by the emperor's *genius* functioned as loyalty tests. They proved you were a faithful subject.

For most Romans, worshiping the emperor was not controversial. You were already worshiping dozens of gods; one more posed no problem. It was patriotic rather than religious in the modern sense. You honored Rome's power and success by honoring its leader.

For Christians and Jews, however, the imperial cult was an impossible demand. Their belief in one God forbade worshiping anyone else. Refusing to make offerings to the emperor's *genius* could be interpreted as treason, as it was evidence of disloyalty to Roman authority.

Even so, the reality of Christian persecution was more complex than simply refusing to worship the emperor. Persecutions varied enormously by time, place, and circumstance. Sometimes Christians were targeted for refusing civic rituals. Often, they were scapegoated for disasters because their refusal to honor traditional gods was believed to anger those gods and bring divine punishment on the community. Local officials might persecute Christians to appease crowds demanding action after a crisis, even without direct imperial orders. Some emperors actively persecuted Christians. Others ignored them, and still others protected them. Persecution was sporadic and inconsistent rather than a systematic, empire-wide policy until much later.

For you, a regular Roman, religion means daily offerings to household gods, attending festivals throughout the year, perhaps consulting an oracle or priest for divine guidance, and participating in civic rituals. You might also be initiated into one of the mystery cults, which promise personal salvation and secret knowledge. These cults offer something the traditional Roman religion does not: hope for a good afterlife and a personal relationship with the divine.

Traditional Roman religion offers no clear afterlife. The dead go to a shadowy underworld, where they exist as weak shades. There is no heaven, no reward for virtue, and no eternal punishment for sin. This was why mystery cults—and eventually Christianity—became so appealing. They promised something better than existing forever as a powerless ghost in the darkness.

For most of your life, however, Roman religion is about duty to the gods, to your family, and to your community. You make offerings, attend festivals, and hope the gods remain favorable. And so far, they have been. Rome is the largest and most powerful empire in the world. The gods must be pleased.

## Legions, Laws, and Concrete: The Three Pillars of Roman Power

We have talked about daily life, entertainment, and religion. But what made Rome an empire that dominated the known world for centuries? Three things: a superior military system, a sophisticated legal framework, and engineering that made the impossible routine.

### The Roman Legion: Why Rome's Army Dominated for Centuries

The Roman legion was one of the most successful military organizations in history. Around the 2$^{nd}$ century CE, roughly twenty-five to thirty legions controlled everything from Britain to Mesopotamia, from the Rhine to the Sahara. That was about 150,000 to 180,000 legionaries, plus an equal or larger number of auxiliary troops. It was not a huge army by modern standards, but it was devastatingly effective.

Why? Four reasons: training, discipline, equipment, and engineering.

A legion had about five thousand to six thousand men organized into smaller units commanded by centurions, professional officers who'd risen through the ranks. These centurions were the backbone of the legion. They trained the troops, enforced discipline, and led in battle. They also carried staffs and beat soldiers who screwed up.

Legionaries were all Roman citizens who served twenty to twenty-five years. They got regular pay, land grants when they retired, and citizenship for their children. This created a professional, disciplined force with long-term loyalty to Rome and often to their commanding general, which caused major problems during civil wars.

Training was brutal. Legionaries drilled constantly in formations, weapons handling, and camp construction. They marched twenty to thirty miles a day, carrying sixty to eighty pounds of equipment. New recruits spent months learning to fight in tight formation, follow commands instantly, and maintain discipline when people were trying to kill them.

Equipment was standardized. Segmented plate armor or chain mail provided protection. A large rectangular shield covered most of the body. A short stabbing sword (*gladius*) was designed for close combat. Two javelins (*pila*) had iron shanks that bent on impact. They couldn't be thrown back, and they sometimes pinned enemy shields together.

Tactics emphasized coordination over individual heroics. Legionaries fought in tight formations. They threw javelins to disrupt enemy lines, then advanced with shields and swords, fighting in ranks where discipline beat bravery. The famous "turtle" formation (*testudo*) had soldiers overlapping shields to create a mobile fortress that could approach walls under arrow fire.

Here was the part that amazed other armies: legions built a fortified camp every single night. After marching all day, they dug ditches, built earthwork walls, and constructed a defensible camp. Barbarian armies slept in the open. Romans slept behind fortifications.

Engineering was central to Roman military success. Legionaries built roads, bridges, siege equipment, and fortifications. They were soldiers and engineers. When Caesar besieged Alesia, his legions built double walls—one to trap the Gauls inside and one to keep the relief army outside. When Trajan campaigned in Dacia, his legions built a massive bridge across the Danube. Roman military engineering made operations possible that other armies couldn't even imagine.

Discipline was legendary and brutal. Deserters were executed. Cowardice by a unit could result in decimation; every tenth man would be selected by lot and beaten to death by his fellow soldiers. This was rare, but it demonstrated Rome's absolute commitment to discipline.

This combination of professional troops, superior training, standardized equipment, engineering capability, and brutal discipline made the Roman legion nearly unbeatable. Rome lost battles occasionally, but Rome almost always won wars.

### Roman Law: Why Modern Legal Systems Still Use Roman Ideas

Law was one of Rome's most lasting legacies. Modern legal systems throughout Europe, Latin America, and much of the world have been based on Roman legal principles developed over centuries.

What made Roman law revolutionary? The Romans had written laws that everyone could see. You could actually know what the law required. This was far fairer than systems based on unwritten customs or whatever the ruler felt like that day.

There were also established courts, rules for trials, evidence requirements, and rights for the accused. It wasn't perfect. Trials could be biased, corruption existed, and slaves were tortured for testimony, but there was a system rather than arbitrary justice.

Rome developed jurists, legal experts who studied, interpreted, and wrote about law. Their opinions carried weight and helped develop legal principles. Famous jurists like Gaius and Ulpian wrote treatises that became authoritative.

Roman law had sophisticated rules about property, contracts, inheritance, and obligations. This provided predictability for business and allowed complex commercial relationships. The *Corpus Juris Civilis*, compiled under Byzantine Emperor Justinian in the 6th century CE, preserved Roman legal writings and formed the basis for many modern legal systems. Roman principles, such as "the burden of proof lies with the accuser," influenced modern law.

Of course, Roman law wasn't perfect by modern standards. Slavery was legal and protected. Women had limited rights. Torture was used on slaves. Punishments were brutal. People could be crucified, burned alive, or thrown to wild animals. The law treated people differently based on status.

Still, Roman law provided a framework for resolving disputes, protecting property, and maintaining order across a vast empire. It allowed people in Britain, Egypt, Spain, and Syria to conduct business and resolve disputes under common legal principles. This was essential to Rome's economy and political stability.

## Engineering Marvels: How Rome Built an Empire That's Still Standing

Roman engineering is visible everywhere, even today, two thousand years later. Roman roads served as foundations for modern highways. Roman aqueducts still stand. Some Roman concrete is more durable than modern concrete.

Rome built over 250,000 miles of roads throughout the empire. Major roads like the Appian Way were built in layers with large stones, gravel, and paving stones. They were designed for drainage and durability. Roman roads were straight whenever possible, running directly toward destinations. They included bridges, tunnels, and cut through hills. Milestones marked distances. Way stations provided shelter and supplies.

The Appian Way.[18]

The saying "all roads lead to Rome" was pretty much true. You could travel from Rome to Britain or Egypt while staying on Roman roads nearly the entire way. This road network connected cities, facilitated trade, sped military movements, and integrated the empire.

Aqueducts brought water from miles away. Rome needed massive amounts of water for drinking, baths, fountains, and sewers. The city eventually had eleven major aqueducts bringing water from sources up to fifty miles away. These used gravity flow, maintaining a steady downward grade over dozens of miles. Where valleys required it, massive arched bridges carried the water. The Pont du Gard in France stood 160 feet tall. Many Roman aqueducts still function today.

The Pont du Gard in France.[19]

Clean water was crucial to public health. Roman cities were healthier than medieval cities, partly because of reliable water and sewer systems.

Roman concrete was revolutionary. Made from volcanic ash, lime, and aggregate, it could be poured into forms and even set underwater. The Pantheon in Rome has the world's largest unreinforced concrete dome; it is 142 feet across. It was completed around 125 CE and is still standing and still waterproof.

Roman concrete used *pozzolana*, volcanic ash from near Naples, which reacted with lime to create an incredibly strong material. Some Roman marine concrete actually got stronger over time as seawater reacted with the volcanic ash, creating new minerals that reinforced the structure. Roman harbor installations have lasted two thousand years underwater.

Roman architecture combined Greek aesthetics with engineering innovation. The arch, the vault, and the dome allowed the Romans to build larger, more complex structures than anyone before. Amphitheaters, bath complexes, temples, and aqueducts all used these innovations.

Romans developed concrete faced with brick or stone, allowing them to build quickly on a massive scale. The Colosseum, the Baths of Caracalla, and countless other structures demonstrate Roman architectural ambition and engineering skill.

**Slavery: The Foundation Nobody Talks About**

We need to address the uncomfortable truth. All of this–the legions, the roads, the aqueducts, the games, the prosperity–was built on slavery.

Rome was a slave society. Scholars estimated that during the height of the Roman Republic following major conquests, perhaps 30 to 40 percent of Italy's population were slaves. By the mid-2nd century CE–a period of relative stability–the proportion was likely closer to 20 to 30 percent. In the city of Rome itself, the proportion of slaves remained substantial. Throughout the empire, millions of people were enslaved.

Slaves came from multiple sources. They could be prisoners of war (the largest source), children born to slave mothers, people sold by their parents, kidnapped victims, and people enslaved as punishment for crimes. Roman conquests during the Roman Republic and early empire flooded Italy with slaves. When Rome conquered Carthage, tens of thousands were enslaved. Caesar claimed in his *Commentaries* to have enslaved a million people during his Gallic campaigns–a figure modern historians see as typical military exaggeration, though the actual numbers were still substantial.

Slaves did everything. They worked on the large estates (*latifundia*), which produced grain, wine, and olive oil. They worked in mines and quarries under brutal conditions. Mining was essentially a death sentence, and slaves were worked to death in mines throughout the empire. They worked in workshops producing goods. They also worked as domestic servants in wealthy households, cooking, cleaning, and caring for children.

Some slaves held skilled positions. They could work as teachers, doctors, accountants, and secretaries. Imperial slaves—those owned by the emperor—could hold important administrative posts. Some skilled slaves accumulated money and eventually bought their freedom.

Slavery in Rome was not based on race. Slaves came from all ethnicities and regions. It was based on legal status. A Gaul could be enslaved by Romans, and a Roman could be enslaved by pirates or foreign enemies. Anyone could become a slave through bad luck.

However, this did not make Roman slavery less brutal. Slaves had no legal rights. Masters could punish them however they wanted, including execution. Sexual exploitation of slaves was common and legal. Slaves could not legally marry, and their children were property. They could be sold at any time, separating families. The threat of being sold to the mines or forced to fight as gladiators kept slaves compliant.

Manumission (freeing slaves) was common in Rome compared to some other slave societies. Masters freed slaves for various reasons. It could be a reward for loyal service because the slave bought their freedom or through provisions in the master's will. Freed slaves (*liberti*) became Roman citizens, though with some limitations. Their children were full citizens, which created social mobility that was unavailable in many societies, but it did not make slavery acceptable.

Rome's prosperity depended on slave labor. The grain that fed the city came from estates worked by slaves. The mines that produced silver for coins and metals for weapons used slave labor. The construction projects that beautified cities used slave labor. The workshops that produced goods used slave labor. Roman citizens enjoyed leisure time partly because slaves did much of the work.

When you walked through Rome, enjoying the entertainment, the baths, and the public buildings, you were seeing a civilization built by enslaved people. This was an uncomfortable truth, but it was essential to understanding Rome. The glory, the achievements, the culture—it was all interconnected with the exploitation of millions of enslaved human beings.

# Chapter 8: The Five Good Emperors and the Empire's Peak

If you had to pick one century to live in the Roman Empire, most historians would tell you to pick the $2^{nd}$ century CE. This was Rome's golden age. The empire was at its height, the economy was humming along, cities flourished, and the Mediterranean world experienced unprecedented peace and stability. Was it Rome's absolute peak? Historians argue about that. However, the $2^{nd}$ century CE represented one of humanity's most successful experiments in running a massive empire.

What made this century so special? Five emperors in a row were actually competent and chosen through a system that worked—adoptive succession. Instead of passing power to their biological sons (who might be idiots), these emperors adopted talented men and made them heirs. It was Rome's approach to picking leaders based on merit.

These five emperors were Nerva, Trajan, Hadrian, Antoninus Pius, and Marcus Aurelius. Later historians called them the "Five Good Emperors." Marcus Aurelius broke the system by passing power to his biological son, Commodus, who was not a good ruler. And the golden age ended.

Let's see how it all worked and why it couldn't last.

## The Adoptive Succession: When Rome Figured Out How to Pick Good Emperors

The year 96 CE was messy. Emperor Domitian, the last of the Flavian dynasty, which had ruled since 69 CE, was assassinated by members of his own household. Domitian had become increasingly paranoid and tyrannical, conducting treason trials and executing senators he suspected of disloyalty. His murder was a palace coup, and Rome faced the familiar question of who would be emperor next.

The conspirators chose Nerva, an elderly, respected senator with no military background and no children. He was sixty-six years old. Nerva was a safe, transitional figure who wouldn't threaten anyone and wasn't expected to reign for many years.

However, Nerva faced an immediate problem. The Praetorian Guard was angry that Domitian had been murdered without their approval, and they wanted revenge. Nerva was politically isolated and militarily weak. He needed the support of the legions, and he needed an heir who could command respect from the military.

So, in 97 CE, Nerva did something that established a pattern for the next century. He adopted Marcus Ulpius Traianus (Trajan) as his son and designated heir. Trajan was a successful general commanding legions in Germania, a Roman from a Spanish family, and popular with the troops. When Nerva died in 98 CE after reigning only sixteen months, Trajan succeeded him peacefully. The legions and the Senate accepted him. The transition was smooth.

This established the principle of the emperor choosing the best man available as his successor and adopting him. The heir would be trained in government and military command, proving his abilities before taking power. When the emperor died, the adopted son would succeed without a civil war or dispute.

It sounded simple, but it was revolutionary. This wasn't a formal system or constitutional law. It depended entirely on emperors making wise choices and on lucky circumstances, particularly the lack of biological heirs who might claim precedence. But when it worked, Rome had a way to ensure competent leadership. And for nearly a century, the stars aligned, and emperors chose well.

## Trajan (r. 98–117 CE): The Empire Reaches Its Greatest Extent

Trajan came from a Roman family in Hispania (Spain). This signaled an important shift: the empire was becoming genuinely multi-ethnic, with leadership coming from the provinces, not just old Roman families in Italy.

Ancient sources described Trajan as the ideal emperor. He was militarily successful, brave, respectful toward the Senate, and generous with public spending. The Senate later decreed that each new emperor should be wished to be "luckier than Augustus and better than Trajan," making Trajan the standard for imperial excellence.

Trajan was best known for his military campaigns. Between 101 and 106 CE, he fought two wars against Dacia (roughly modern Romania), a wealthy kingdom north of the Danube that had previously defeated Roman armies. The Dacian Wars were brutal, large-scale campaigns involving multiple legions fighting in difficult terrain.

The wars were documented in extraordinary detail on Trajan's Column in Rome, which was completed in 113 CE. This 125-foot-tall marble column depicted the campaigns in a continuous spiral frieze with over 2,500 figures—soldiers marching, building fortifications, fighting battles, besieging cities, and accepting surrender. It is one of our best sources for how Roman armies actually looked and operated.

The Dacian Wars ended with a complete Roman victory. The Dacian king Decebalus committed suicide rather than be captured. Dacia became a Roman province, and its gold mines filled Rome's treasury. Ancient sources claimed Trajan brought back enormous quantities of gold. This wealth funded massive building projects in Rome and throughout the empire.

Trajan used the Dacian gold to transform Rome. He built Trajan's Forum in Rome, the largest and most elaborate of the imperial forums. This massive complex included a basilica (the Basilica Ulpia), two libraries (one for Latin texts and one for Greek), a monumental column, and Trajan's Market—a multi-story commercial complex that is sometimes called the world's first shopping mall, though it was more complex than that, including administrative offices and storage facilities.

**Trajan's Market today.**[80]

Trajan's Forum was architectural propaganda. It celebrated his military victories while demonstrating Rome's wealth and sophistication. The Basilica Ulpia was the largest basilica in Rome, with enormous granite columns imported from Egypt. The libraries housed Rome's greatest collection of scrolls and codices. The whole complex was faced with marble and decorated with sculptures and reliefs showing Roman superiority over barbarians.

But Trajan did not just build in Rome. Throughout the empire, he funded infrastructure projects: roads connecting provinces, bridges spanning rivers that had hindered commerce, harbors improving maritime trade, and aqueducts bringing water to growing cities. In Alcántara, Spain, a bridge he built in 106 CE still stands and carries traffic today.

Trajan also enhanced social welfare in Italy through the *alimenta* program–a system in which the imperial treasury loaned money to farmers at low interest rates. The interest payments funded stipends for poor children. This was not charity in the modern sense but a program to ensure Italy's agricultural productivity while supporting the freeborn population.

Ancient sources also praised Trajan for his accessible, modest personal style despite his absolute power. Pliny the Younger, who served under Trajan, described an emperor who consulted the Senate respectfully, who did not surround himself with excessive luxury, and who was approachable to ordinary citizens. Whether this reflected reality or was propaganda is debatable, but it showed the ideal against which Romans measured emperors.

But Trajan's ambitions were not satisfied with Dacia. Between 113 and 117 CE, he launched a war against the Parthian Empire in the east. Rome and Parthia had fought on and off for over a century, with neither side achieving a decisive victory. Trajan wanted to succeed where others had failed and conquer Mesopotamia.

The Parthian War started well. Roman forces conquered Armenia, then advanced into Mesopotamia, capturing Ctesiphon, the Parthian capital. Trajan reached the Persian Gulf, the farthest east any Roman emperor had campaigned. In 116 CE, the Roman Empire reached its maximum territorial extent, stretching from Scotland to Mesopotamia, from the Atlantic to the Persian Gulf.

The greatest extent of the Roman Empire.[21]

But of course, conquering territory was different from holding it. The newly conquered regions revolted almost immediately. Jewish populations in Cyprus, Egypt, and Cyrenaica (eastern part of Libya) rebelled in what is known as the Kitos War or the Diaspora Revolt (115–117 CE). Whether these uprisings were coordinated responses to Trajan's Mesopotamian campaign or separate revolts with different local causes has been debated by historians, but they stretched Roman forces dangerously thin. Trajan had to send legions to suppress these uprisings while trying to hold Mesopotamia.

Then Trajan's health failed. He fell seriously ill in 117 CE, possibly from a stroke. He began withdrawing from Mesopotamia, recognizing that Rome could not hold these eastern conquests. Trajan died in August 117 CE in Cilicia (southern Turkey) on the journey back to Rome. He was sixty-three years old.

Before dying, Trajan allegedly adopted Hadrian, his cousin and ward, as his successor. It is possible that Hadrian's wife, Plotina, forged the document, as the announcement came very close to Trajan's death. Hadrian commanded legions in Syria, and the army supported him, so the Senate quickly confirmed him as emperor.

Hadrian immediately abandoned most of Trajan's conquests. Mesopotamia was given up, and Armenia became a client kingdom again. The empire returned to roughly the borders it had held before Trajan's eastern wars. Modern historians interpreted this as strategic realism. Rome could not sustainably defend and govern these territories. Whether Hadrian understood something Trajan had not, whether circumstances had changed, or whether the two emperors simply had different strategic philosophies was debated, the effect was clear. The empire contracted to what Hadrian saw as more defensible frontiers.

**Hadrian (r. 117–138 CE): The Emperor Who Built Walls and Loved Greece**

Hadrian was almost the opposite of Trajan in temperament and priorities. Where Trajan was a soldier who loved campaigning, Hadrian was an intellectual who loved Greek culture, architecture, and philosophy. Where Trajan expanded the empire aggressively, Hadrian focused on consolidating and defending what Rome already held.

Hadrian spent more than half his reign traveling throughout the empire. No emperor before or since traveled as extensively. He visited nearly every province, inspecting fortifications, meeting with local officials, settling disputes, and overseeing construction projects. Ancient sources suggested he traveled approximately eleven years out of his twenty-one-year reign—an extraordinary amount of time away from Rome.

These journeys were not tourism. Hadrian was inspecting and strengthening the empire's frontiers. He believed Rome had reached its natural limits and that future policy should focus on defending borders, not expanding them. This was a fundamental shift from centuries of Roman expansion.

The most famous result of this defensive policy was Hadrian's Wall in Britain, which was built between 122 and 128 CE. This massive stone fortification stretched seventy-three miles across northern Britain, from coast to coast, marking the northernmost frontier of the empire. The wall was about fifteen to twenty feet tall, with a deep ditch on the northern side, milecastles (small forts) every Roman mile, and larger forts at intervals. Thousands of soldiers garrisoned the wall, controlling movement between Roman Britain and the unconquered lands to the north.

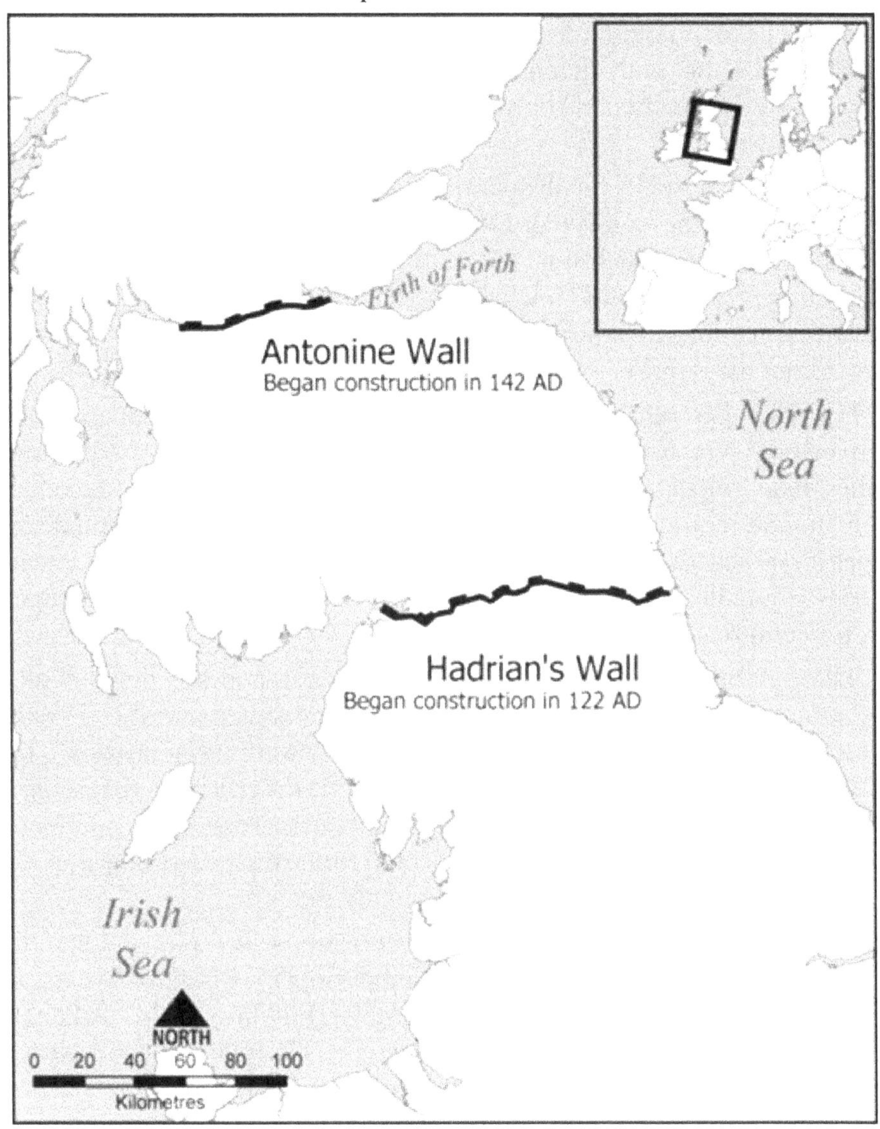


**Map of Hadrian's Wall and the Antonine Wall.**[22]

Hadrian's Wall was not primarily a military barrier in the sense of stopping armies, as a determined force could eventually overcome it. Its purposes were to control and monitor movement across the frontier, collect customs duties on trade, project Roman power into unconquered territories, and provide a clear, dramatic boundary between Roman civilization and the barbarian lands beyond.

Hadrian built similar frontier fortifications elsewhere. In Germania, he constructed a wooden palisade and earthwork barrier called the Limes Germanicus, defining the frontier between the Rhine and the Danube. In North Africa, he built defensive works in the Sahara. Throughout the empire, he strengthened border fortifications and improved military infrastructure.

But Hadrian was equally famous for his cultural projects. He was deeply philhellenic–a lover of Greek culture–to the point that he wore a Greek-style beard, which was unusual for Romans, who were traditionally clean-shaven (the beard might also have concealed skin blemishes, according to ancient sources). He commissioned magnificent buildings throughout the empire, especially in Athens and Rome.

Hadrian also reformed imperial administration. He regularized the bureaucracy, creating a professional civil service staffed by equestrians rather than relying on senatorial aristocrats or freedmen. He codified Roman law, commissioning the jurist Salvius Julianus to compile the Praetor's Edict–the body of case law that governed Roman legal practice. This became the foundation for later legal codes and influenced European law for centuries.

These reforms made the empire more efficient and less dependent on the emperor. Provinces were governed more systematically. Taxation became more predictable. Legal procedures were standardized. This might seem like boring bureaucratic stuff, but it was crucial to managing an empire of fifty to sixty million people spread across three continents. Hadrian understood that one man could not run everything and that institutions needed to function independently.

In Athens, Hadrian completed the enormous Temple of Olympian Zeus, which had been under construction for over six hundred years. He built libraries, aqueducts, and other public buildings. The Athenians honored him as a new founder of their city. Hadrian saw himself as a patron of Greek culture and a protector of classical civilization.

In Rome, Hadrian built his most famous monument, the Pantheon. The original Pantheon had been built by Agrippa in the 20s BCE but had burned down. Hadrian rebuilt it completely between 118 and 128 CE, creating one of the most extraordinary buildings in history. The Pantheon's dome—142 feet in diameter—is the largest unreinforced concrete dome in the world. It is still standing today, nearly 1,900 years later. It is one of the best-preserved Roman buildings and is still used as a church.

The Pantheon's dome.[28]

Hadrian also built an enormous villa complex at Tivoli, just outside Rome. Hadrian's Villa was a vast estate covering about 250 acres, with palaces, temples, theaters, libraries, bathhouses, and gardens designed to recreate famous buildings and landscapes from throughout the empire, especially from Greece and Egypt. It was Hadrian's personal retreat, where he could surround himself with beauty and culture.

However, Hadrian's reign was not all peaceful construction. In 132 CE, Judaea erupted in revolt—the Bar Kokhba Revolt, named after its leader, Simon bar Kokhba, who claimed to be the messiah. The causes included religious tensions, economic grievances, and Hadrian's plan to build a Roman colony on the site of Jerusalem with a temple to Jupiter on the Temple Mount.

The revolt was massive and well organized. Jewish forces controlled much of Judaea for three years. Rome sent multiple legions and some of its best generals. The fighting was brutal. The ancient historian Cassius Dio claimed that 580,000 Jews were killed and 50 Judean fortified towns and 985 villages were destroyed. Modern historians view these figures as likely exaggerated or symbolic of the scale of destruction rather than precise counts, but they still indicate enormous casualties and devastation.

Rome won, but at a terrible cost. Entire legions were lost. The province of Judaea was devastated. After the revolt, Hadrian expelled Jews from Jerusalem, which he rebuilt as a Roman colony called Aelia Capitolina. The province was renamed Syria Palaestina, deliberately erasing the name Judaea. The Jewish population was decimated, and the religious and cultural center of Judaism was destroyed. It would take until the 20th century for Jews to regain political sovereignty in their ancestral homeland.

Hadrian's personal life was also marked by tragedy. He had no children with his wife, Sabina. Their marriage was reportedly cold and unhappy. But Hadrian had a passionate relationship with a young Greek man named Antinous. In 130 CE, while traveling in Egypt, Antinous drowned in the Nile River. The circumstances were mysterious; ancient sources suggested suicide, accident, or even ritual sacrifice. Hadrian was devastated.

He had Antinous declared a god and established a cult in his honor. Cities throughout the empire built temples to Antinous. Hundreds of statues were created—more than survive of any other private individual from antiquity. Hadrian founded a city at the site of Antinous's death called Antinoopolis.

Hadrian's later years were difficult. He suffered from poor health and became increasingly suspicious and cruel. He executed several senators and officials, alienating the Senate. When choosing his successor, he adopted Antoninus in 138 CE with the condition that Antoninus would adopt two younger men: Marcus Aurelius (Hadrian's great-nephew) and Lucius Verus. Hadrian was planning succession two generations ahead.

Hadrian died in July 138 CE at the age of sixty-two. He was ill and reportedly in great pain. Ancient sources suggested he begged his servants to kill him to end his suffering, but they refused. He composed a famous short poem just before his death:

"Little soul, wandering, gentle,

Guest and companion of the body,

To what places will you now go,

Pale, stiff, naked,

Unable to play as you used to?"

It was a poignant meditation on mortality from a man who had seen more of the world than perhaps any other person in antiquity.

### Antoninus Pius (r. 138–161 CE): The Peaceful Emperor

Antoninus Pius is the least famous of the Five Good Emperors, probably because his reign was peaceful and relatively uneventful. After the dramatic building projects of Trajan and Hadrian and the constant travel and frontier wars, Antoninus's reign seems almost boring. But boring is good when you're ruling an empire.

Antoninus was fifty-one when he became emperor and ruled for twenty-three years—one of the longest reigns in Roman history. Ancient sources describe him as conscientious, moderate, and respectful of the Senate. He was given the title "Pius" (dutiful or devoted) because of his efforts to ensure Hadrian's deification. The Senate had been reluctant because Hadrian had executed senators in his final years, but Antoninus insisted on honoring his adoptive father.

Unlike Hadrian, Antoninus didn't travel. He spent his entire reign in Italy, mostly in Rome or at imperial villas. He was essentially a peacetime administrator, managing the empire efficiently without dramatic initiatives.

The empire prospered under Antoninus, though some frontier areas faced persistent pressures even during this relatively peaceful period. Overall, trade flourished in the empire's core regions. Cities grew. The frontiers remained mostly peaceful, with only minor campaigns, the most significant being the construction of the Antonine Wall in Scotland around 142 CE. This pushed the Roman frontier north of Hadrian's Wall. However, the Antonine Wall was abandoned within twenty years, and the frontier returned to Hadrian's Wall, suggesting the northern expansion wasn't sustainable.

Antoninus managed imperial finances conservatively. He didn't undertake massive building projects like his predecessors. He lowered taxes when possible and left a full treasury to his successors. His reign demonstrated that Rome could function peacefully and prosperously under competent administration.

Marcus Aurelius, Antoninus's adopted son, spent these years being trained for power. He held consular positions, learned government administration, and studied philosophy with the best teachers in Rome. When Antoninus died peacefully in 161 CE at the age of seventy-four, Marcus was prepared to rule. The succession was smooth, as the adoptive system intended.

**Marcus Aurelius (r. 161–180 CE): The Philosopher King Who Spent His Life at War**

Marcus Aurelius is probably the most famous of the Five Good Emperors today, largely because his personal philosophical writings, the *Meditations*, survived and became one of the most influential works of Stoic philosophy. He's the ideal of the "philosopher king" that Plato described. Marcus Aurelius was a ruler who loved wisdom, sought virtue, and governed with justice.

The irony is that Marcus Aurelius spent almost his entire reign at war. The philosopher who wanted to live a life of contemplation and virtue spent nearly twenty years on military campaigns on the frontiers, fighting enemies who threatened the empire's survival.

Marcus made an unusual decision immediately after becoming emperor. He shared power with his adoptive brother, Lucius Verus, making him co-emperor. This was unprecedented. Rome had never had two equal emperors ruling simultaneously (Hadrian's proposal of this was more theoretical). Marcus and Lucius ruled together from 161 to 169 CE, until Lucius died.

Almost immediately after their accession, Rome faced crises on multiple frontiers. In the east, the Parthian Empire invaded Armenia and Syria in 161 CE, defeating Roman forces and threatening Rome's eastern provinces. Lucius Verus was sent east with reinforcements. The war lasted until 166 CE, with Roman forces eventually defeating Parthia. However, Roman soldiers returning from the east brought back something more dangerous than Parthian soldiers: a plague.

The Antonine Plague, which began in 165, was likely smallpox or measles. It devastated the empire for over a decade, killing millions.

Ancient sources describe cities emptied of inhabitants and mass funeral pyres. The historian Cassius Dio and the physician Galen both describe the plague's symptoms and devastating impact. Estimates suggest the plague killed anywhere from five to ten million people, which was perhaps a tenth of the empire's population.

The plague's effects went beyond immediate deaths. Agricultural production declined as farmers died, leading to food shortages. Tax revenues fell as populations shrank, straining imperial finances. Trade networks were disrupted as merchants and ship crews died. The Roman army was so depleted that Marcus had to recruit gladiators and even bandits to fill the ranks, showing how desperate the manpower situation had become. Some historians argue that the Antonine Plague marked the beginning of Rome's decline, weakening the empire's demographic and economic foundations as external pressures increased.

While the empire was weakening from the plague, Germanic tribes along the Rhine and Danube frontiers saw an opportunity. The Marcomannic Wars began in 166 CE and would continue for most of Marcus's reign. Germanic and Sarmatian tribes crossed the Danube in massive numbers. They were not just raiding. They were migrating and seeking land to settle.

In 167, Germanic tribes invaded Italy itself for the first time in over 250 years, reaching Aquileia in northeastern Italy. This was a shocking violation of Italy's sanctity. Italy was supposed to be safe, far from barbarian threats. Marcus rushed north with legions to repel the invasion.

The Marcomannic Wars were a grinding series of campaigns along the Danube frontier. Marcus spent years living in military camps, commanding armies in the field, negotiating with tribal leaders, and trying to stabilize a frontier that seemed constantly on the verge of collapse. These were not glorious conquests like Trajan's Dacian Wars. These were defensive wars of survival aimed at preventing barbarian tribes from overrunning Roman provinces.

During these long campaigns on the Danube, Marcus wrote his *Meditations*, personal philosophical reflections in Greek. The *Meditations* are remarkable for their Stoic philosophy (a school of thought emphasizing virtue, self-control, and accepting what you cannot change) and their humility. Marcus reminds himself constantly to be virtuous, to accept fate, to not be corrupted by power, to serve others, and to remember his own mortality.

Here are some of the more famous passages:

"You have power over your mind–not outside events. Realize this, and you will find strength."

"Waste no more time arguing about what a good man should be. Be one."

"When you arise in the morning, think of what a precious privilege it is to be alive–to breathe, to think, to enjoy, to love."

"The impediment to action advances action. What stands in the way becomes the way."

These are the thoughts of a man who had absolute power but saw it as a burden. He wanted to be wise and good despite being emperor and was fighting wars he didn't want while longing for philosophical contemplation. The *Meditations* reveal a deeply human figure struggling with duty, mortality, and the gap between ideals and reality.

Lucius Verus died in 169 CE, possibly from the plague. Marcus continued ruling alone. The wars dragged on. By the late 170s, Marcus had achieved some success. The Germanic tribes were defeated, and the frontier seemed temporarily stable. Some ancient sources suggest Marcus Aurelius planned to annex territories beyond the Danube, creating a new province of Marcomannia.

However, in 180, Marcus Aurelius fell ill and died at the age of fifty-eight in a military camp at Vindobona (modern Vienna) while still on campaign. He had spent nearly his entire reign at war, never achieving the peace he desired. His death is often seen as the end of the Pax Romana, the long peace that had characterized the 2nd century, though peace and prosperity continued in many regions. What's clear is that after 180, the empire faced increasing military pressures, political instability, and economic challenges that the rulers of the 2nd century had largely avoided.

This was because Marcus passed power to his biological son, Commodus. Marcus had no real choice. Commodus was his only surviving son, and passing over him would have risked civil war. But Commodus was not chosen for ability. He was heir by birth, and he would prove disastrously unfit for power.

### Commodus (r. 180–192 CE): When the System Broke

Commodus became emperor at age eighteen. Unlike the previous emperors, who had been trained in government and military command for years before taking power, Commodus was young, inexperienced, and had spent his life as an imperial prince with few serious responsibilities.

Ancient sources describe Commodus as lazy, cruel, and obsessed with gladiatorial combat. He reportedly fought in the arena himself. He dressed as a gladiator, killing animals and fighting carefully arranged matches against opponents who were ordered not to harm him. He saw himself as Hercules reborn and had statues made depicting him dressed as the hero, with a lion's skin and club.

This was scandalous. Emperors were supposed to be dignified and serious. They might attend the games, but they didn't perform in them. Gladiators were *infames*—legally disgraced people. For an emperor to fight as a gladiator humiliated the imperial office and horrified the senatorial class.

Commodus also renamed Rome itself "Colonia Commodiana" (the Colony of Commodus). He renamed the months of the year after his own titles. He wanted the Senate renamed "Commodian Senate." This megalomania went beyond normal imperial self-aggrandizement into what ancient sources portrayed as insanity.

However, we must note that ancient sources on Commodus are heavily biased. They were written by senators who hated him and had every reason to portray him in the worst possible light. Modern historians debate whether Commodus was genuinely unstable or whether some of his actions were provocative attacks on senatorial privilege. By fighting as a gladiator, Commodus was rejecting the Senate's values and appealing to the common people, who loved gladiatorial combat. This might have been calculated political theater rather than madness. The truth likely lies somewhere between the characterization of a mad tyrant and a strategic ruler. Commodus appears to have been both impulsive and calculating, both cruel and crowd-pleasing.

Regardless of his motivations, Commodus's reign was disastrous for governance. He delegated the actual administration to praetorian prefects and favorites who became corrupt and abusive. He executed senators he suspected of disloyalty. He debased the currency to fund his lavish lifestyle and games. The government that had functioned smoothly under the Five Good Emperors began to break down.

In 192, conspirators, including Commodus's mistress Marcia and the Praetorian prefect, planned his assassination. They tried to poison him, but he vomited up the poison. So, they sent a wrestler named Narcissus to strangle him in his bath. Commodus was thirty-one years old; he died after twelve years of increasingly erratic rule.

His death triggered a civil war. Multiple generals proclaimed themselves emperor. The Year of the Five Emperors (193 CE) saw rapid turnover until Septimius Severus emerged victorious in 197, establishing a new dynasty. The golden age was over.

From peaks, there's only one direction to go.

**A bust of Septimius Severus.**[24]

# Chapter 9: The Third-Century Crisis: Fifty Years of Chaos That Nearly Destroyed Rome

The assassination of Commodus in 192 didn't restore the golden age. Instead, it triggered a civil war. Multiple generals proclaimed themselves emperor. Armies fought each other across the empire. After a year of chaos, Septimius Severus emerged victorious in 197, establishing the Severan dynasty. The Severans ruled for about forty years, maintaining some stability, though their reigns were marked by military campaigns, increased taxation, and growing reliance on the army.

In 235, when the last Severan emperor was murdered by his own troops, something broke. The next fifty years—from 235 to 284—saw the Roman Empire nearly collapse. This period is called the Crisis of the Third Century, and it was one of the worst sustained catastrophes in Roman history. The empire faced simultaneous military invasions, economic collapse, devastating plagues, political chaos, and the near-total breakdown of central authority.

Ancient sources from this period are fragmentary and confusing, which makes sense. When your civilization is falling apart, keeping detailed historical records isn't the priority. But we can piece together what happened. What we know is that a disaster came terrifyingly close to ending the Roman Empire forever.

## The Barracks Emperors: When Soldiers Decided Who Ruled Rome

The fundamental problem was simple: the Roman army had learned it could make emperors and unmake them.

When Maximinus Thrax became emperor in 235 after his soldiers murdered Severus Alexander, he set a precedent. Maximinus wasn't a senator. He wasn't from a noble family. He wasn't even Italian; ancient sources describe him as a Thracian (from roughly modern Bulgaria) of low birth. He was supposedly a former shepherd who joined the army and rose through the ranks. His elevation showed that military force alone could create an emperor.

This broke what little remained of the adoptive system's principle that emperors should be chosen for ability and legitimacy. Now, any general with enough loyal troops could proclaim himself emperor. And many did.

Between 235 and 284, ancient sources record that somewhere between fifty and seventy men claimed the title of emperor. This figure includes all regional usurpers and generals proclaimed by single military units; the number of emperors widely accepted by large factions or the Senate was closer to twenty or thirty. Regardless of the exact count, the turnover was extraordinary. Most reigned for less than a year. Many were murdered by their own soldiers. A few died in battle against foreign enemies. Almost none died peacefully.

These emperors are sometimes called the "Barracks emperors" because they were made by soldiers in military camps, not through any legitimate succession process. The pattern was depressingly predictable:

1. An emperor leads troops on campaign.
2. The campaign goes badly, the emperor doesn't pay his soldiers enough, or the troops just get bored.
3. Soldiers murder the emperor and proclaim their general as the new emperor.
4. Other armies hear about this and proclaim their own generals as emperor.
5. Civil war breaks out as rival claimants fight for supremacy.
6. Eventually, someone wins and becomes emperor.
7. Within months or years, the cycle repeats.

This sounds almost comical in its absurdity, but the consequences were catastrophic. Every civil war meant Roman armies were fighting each other instead of defending frontiers. Every murdered emperor meant disrupted administration and broken treaties. Every new claimant needed money to pay his troops, so taxation increased, and the currency was debased. The empire was consuming itself.

Some examples show just how chaotic it became:

**Gordian I and Gordian II (238 CE):** This father and son duo were proclaimed co-emperors in Africa. They reigned for twenty-two days before both of them died. Gordian II was killed in battle, and Gordian I committed suicide when he heard the news.

**Pupienus and Balbinus (238 CE):** The Senate appointed these two as co-emperors to oppose Maximinus Thrax. They reigned for ninety-nine days before the Praetorian Guard murdered them both.

**Philip the Arab (244–249 CE):** He was a relatively successful emperor who celebrated Rome's one-thousandth anniversary in 248 CE with massive games. He was murdered by his own troops the following year.

**Decius (249–251 CE):** He launched the first empire-wide persecution of Christians, trying to restore the traditional Roman religion and unity. He was killed fighting Goths at the Battle of Abritus, making him the first Roman emperor killed in battle by foreign enemies in centuries.

**Valerian (253–260 CE):** He was captured by the Sasanian Persian Empire in 260 CE; he was allegedly used as a footstool by the Persian king. Valerian was the only Roman emperor ever captured alive by a foreign enemy. He died in captivity, a humiliation Rome had never experienced before.

**Gallienus (253–268 CE):** He ruled for fifteen years, making this one of the longest reigns of the period. He was murdered by his own officers during a siege.

The rapid turnover created chaos. New emperors couldn't learn the job before being killed. Policies changed constantly. Nobody could plan for the long term when the government might collapse next month. The empire lost any coherent direction.

### The Frontiers Collapse: When Everyone Attacked at Once

While Romans were killing each other, Rome's enemies noticed the chaos and attacked.

The northern frontiers—the Rhine and Danube regions that had held for centuries—collapsed. Germanic tribes poured across the rivers in massive numbers. These weren't just raids anymore. Entire peoples were migrating, seeking land and plunder, and pushing into Roman territory.

The Alemanni invaded Italy in 259 CE in a raid that reached the Milan area before being defeated. Germanic tribes raided Gaul repeatedly, devastating cities and the countryside. The Goths crossed the Lower Danube, invaded the Balkans, and even launched naval raids into the Aegean Sea. Athens was sacked by a Germanic tribe in 267. The unthinkable was happening—Athens, the cultural heart of the classical world, was being pillaged by barbarians.

In the east, the situation was even worse. The Sasanian Empire, a new, aggressive Persian dynasty that had overthrown the Parthians, proved far more formidable than the Parthians had been. The Sasanians were militarily sophisticated, ideologically motivated (they promoted Zoroastrianism as the state religion), and determined to reconquer territories they considered rightfully Persian.

Between 241 and 272, the Sasanians repeatedly invaded Roman territory. They captured and sacked cities, took prisoners, and extracted tribute. The capture of Valerian in 260 was a spectacular Sasanian success. Persian armies under King Shapur I captured Antioch (one of Rome's largest cities) and raided deep into Roman territory. Roman forces were stretched so thin that defending one frontier meant abandoning another.

Then the empire fragmented into semi-independent polities.

In 260, the western provinces—Gaul, Britain, and Spain—broke away and formed the Gallic Empire under Postumus, a general who had been defending the Rhine frontier. Postumus wasn't trying to conquer Rome or reject Roman identity; he claimed to be protecting the western provinces since the central government couldn't. He maintained Roman institutions and framed his rule as temporary until Rome could recover. The Gallic Empire had its own emperors, armies, and administration. It lasted until 274.

Around the same time, the city of Palmyra in Syria became effectively independent under Queen Zenobia. Palmyra was a wealthy trading city that had been a Roman ally. When Rome couldn't defend the east, Palmyra's forces stepped into the power vacuum, conquering Egypt around 270, along with Syria and parts of Asia Minor, creating the Palmyrene Empire. Zenobia styled herself as a Roman empress and claimed to be protecting Roman territories from Persian invasion. She was not rejecting Rome but filling the void Rome had left.

By 270, the "Roman Empire" consisted of three competing polities: the central empire ruled from Rome, the Gallic Empire in the west, and the

Palmyrene Empire in the east. Rome controlled only Italy, the Balkans, and North Africa. The empire that had dominated the Mediterranean for centuries had fragmented into competing states. Complete collapse seemed imminent.

The Roman Empire, the Gallic Empire, and the Palmyrene Empire.[25]

## The Economy Collapses: When Money Stopped Being Money

The economic crisis worsened the military disaster. The empire's financial system, which had been relatively stable for centuries, completely broke down.

The core problem was that the emperors needed money to pay their armies, but the empire's tax base was shrinking as provinces were devastated by war and plague. The solution the emperors adopted was to debase the currency—reduce the precious-metal content of coins while maintaining the same face value.

Roman silver coins (*denarii*) had historically contained about 95 percent silver. By the 230s, this had dropped to about 50 percent. By the 260s, the silver content had dropped to 5 percent. By the 270s, what had once been silver coins were basically bronze coins with a thin silver wash. You could rub the silver coating off with your fingers.

This caused catastrophic inflation. When merchants realized coins contained almost no precious metal, they raised prices—a lot. Ancient sources and surviving data suggest that prices increased perhaps 1,000 percent or more over the 3rd century.

Imagine you're a Roman trying to buy bread in 260 CE. The baker won't accept coins at face value because everyone knows they're worthless. You need to bring huge quantities of debased coins to buy basic necessities. A loaf of bread that cost one denarius in 200 CE might cost many times that amount in 270. And the baker might refuse coins entirely, demanding payment in grain or goods.

The government tried to address this by issuing coins with even higher face values, which just made inflation worse. Ancient sources describe soldiers refusing debased coins and demanding payment in goods, gold, or land instead. Army mutinies sometimes erupted over worthless pay. Tax collectors couldn't collect taxes in worthless currency, so they demanded payment in grain, goods, or services—a return to payment in kind rather than monetized taxation.

Long-distance trade declined dramatically. Why ship goods across the Mediterranean if the money you'll be paid in is worthless by the time you arrive? Cities that had prospered from trade contracted. The complex urban economy simplified into local subsistence agriculture and production.

Government spending collapsed. The emperors couldn't afford to maintain roads, aqueducts, or public buildings. The infrastructure that had taken centuries to build deteriorated in decades. Cities that couldn't maintain their water supplies or grain imports shrank significantly. Some smaller settlements were abandoned entirely as people fled to larger, more defensible urban centers or to rural estates. The urban landscape was transforming, with cities building defensive walls (like Rome's Aurelian Walls) and prioritizing survival over prosperity.

Wealthy people who had invested in property, businesses, and trade saw their fortunes collapse. The middle classes were wiped out. The poor, who had little to lose, became even more desperate. Social mobility disappeared. The Roman world was becoming poorer, simpler, and more desperate.

### The Plague Returns: When Disease Compounded Disaster

As if military invasions and economic collapse weren't enough, plague struck repeatedly during the 3rd century.

We don't know exactly what disease it was, although it was likely smallpox, measles, or possibly both in successive waves. Ancient sources describe symptoms consistent with these diseases, such as fever, pustules, blindness, and death. The Plague of Cyprian, named after a bishop who described it, ravaged the empire from approximately 249 to 262 CE. Cities reported thousands of deaths daily at its peak.

The plague killed indiscriminately. Rich and poor, soldiers and civilians, young and old—all died. The population declined significantly, though exact figures are unknown. Some estimates suggest the plague killed 20 to 30 percent of the empire's population over the course of the 3rd century, though this is highly speculative.

The demographic impact was catastrophic. Farmers died, leading to abandoned farmland and reduced food production. Artisans died, disrupting the production of goods. Soldiers died, weakening the army at the worst possible time. Tax collectors couldn't collect from the dead, further reducing imperial revenue.

The psychological impact was equally severe. Living through repeated plague outbreaks while watching your civilization collapse creates despair. Ancient sources describe cities emptied of inhabitants, bodies lying unburied in streets, and survivors fleeing to the countryside. The traditional religion seemed powerless. It was clear that the gods weren't protecting Rome. This created a spiritual crisis that made people receptive to new religious movements promising salvation and meaning in a chaotic world.

**The Soldier-Emperors Save Rome (Temporarily)**

Yet somehow, the empire survived. Between 268 and 284, a series of tough, competent military commanders, mostly from Illyria (roughly the Balkans), stabilized the situation and began the recovery process. These "Illyrian emperors" or "soldier-emperors" weren't cultured, educated aristocrats. They were hardened military professionals who spent their reigns fighting on the frontiers.

Claudius II took power in 268 CE and immediately faced a massive Gothic invasion. At the Battle of Naissus in 269, Roman forces slaughtered tens of thousands of Goths. Claudius earned the title "Gothicus" for this triumph. However, the plague killed him in 270 after only two years as emperor.

His successor, Aurelian, was perhaps the most significant emperor of the crisis period. A brilliant general and ruthless pragmatist, Aurelian understood that Rome couldn't hold everything. In 271, he made the painful decision to abandon Dacia, the province Trajan had conquered 165 years earlier. The Danube would be the frontier again. This strategic withdrawal shortened the defensive line and freed up troops for more critical fronts.

Then Aurelian set about reunifying the empire. In 272, he marched east against Palmyra. Queen Zenobia's forces fought hard, but Roman discipline and Aurelian's tactical skill won out. Palmyra fell. Zenobia was captured and brought to Rome in triumph, paraded through the streets in golden chains. Aurelian later granted her a villa and pension rather than executing her. The eastern provinces were Roman again.

In 274, Aurelian turned west and defeated the Gallic Empire. After fourteen years of fragmentation, the Roman Empire was whole again under one emperor. Contemporaries called Aurelian "Restorer of the World" (*Restitutor Orbis*).

Aurelian also did something that would have been unthinkable two centuries earlier: he built walls around Rome. The Aurelian Walls were twelve miles long, twenty feet high, and still stand today. They were designed to protect the eternal city from barbarian invasions that might reach Italy itself. The fact that Rome needed walls showed how much had changed. Aurelian also reformed the currency, issuing new coins with higher precious metal content. He couldn't fully fix the inflation, but he stabilized it.

**A section of the Aurelian Walls today.**[36]

In 275, officers murdered Aurelian based on a forged document suggesting he planned to execute them. It seems even successful emperors couldn't escape the cycle of military violence.

Probus continued Aurelian's work when he took power in 276. He defeated Germanic tribes, repelled Sasanian incursions, and secured the frontiers. He attempted to restore discipline in the army by making soldiers help with civilian construction projects, which included building roads, draining marshes, and planting vineyards. The troops resented doing non-military labor. In 282, they murdered him.

The next emperor, Carus, campaigned successfully against the Sasanians and reached the Persian capital, Ctesiphon. Then, in 283, he died mysteriously. He might have been struck by lightning or murdered. His sons, Carinus and Numerian, divided the empire between them. Numerian died in 284; he was possibly murdered. Carinus was defeated and killed in battle by Diocles, an obscure Dalmatian general who proclaimed himself emperor and took the name Diocletian.

These soldier-emperors had accomplished something remarkable. They had beaten back invasions, reunified the empire, and restored some order. However, they had only treated the symptoms, not the causes. How could one emperor defend frontiers stretching thousands of miles? How could the government function when emperors kept being murdered? How could the economy recover when currency was worthless and trade had collapsed?

The empire needed fundamental reform. And Diocletian would provide it.

### Diocletian's Solution: Dividing the Empire to Save It

Diocletian reigned from 284 to 305 CE. He was a brilliant administrator who understood that the empire's problems required systemic solutions, not just military force.

His most radical innovation was the Tetrarchy, the "rule of four." In 286, Diocletian appointed Maximian as co-emperor, with both holding the title Augustus, and divided the empire administratively. Diocletian ruled the East from Nicomedia in Asia Minor. Maximian ruled the West from Milan. They were not splitting the empire permanently; they were colleagues sharing power.

Then, in 293, Diocletian created the Tetrarchy. Each Augustus appointed a junior emperor called a Caesar, who governed part of his territory and would eventually succeed him. Diocletian appointed Galerius as his Caesar in the East. Maximian appointed Constantius Chlorus as his Caesar in the West. Four emperors now ruled cooperatively, each responsible for defending part of the empire's frontiers.

This solved several problems at once. Militarily, four emperors meant four mobile courts and four field armies. When the Germanic tribes threatened the Rhine, Constantius could respond immediately. When the Persians invaded Syria, Galerius handled it. The empire could now defend multiple frontiers simultaneously instead of rushing one emperor back and forth.

The Caesars were the designated heirs. They were trained in government and military command for years before taking power. When the Augusti retired (or died), the Caesars would become the Augusti and appoint new Caesars. This created a structured succession plan that avoided civil wars, at least in theory.

Administratively, the empire was divided into four prefectures, twelve dioceses, and about one hundred provinces. This created smaller, more manageable units. Provincial governors had less power to rebel since they commanded fewer resources and governed smaller territories. Civil and military authority were separated; governors couldn't use troops for rebellion, and military commanders (*duces*) had no civil authority. This reduced the risk of provincial officials accumulating enough power to proclaim themselves emperor.

Diocletian also reformed taxation. He established regular censuses to assess property and population. He created standardized tax assessments based on land productivity and resources, and he imposed new taxes on commerce and professions. These reforms were harsh since taxation increased significantly, but they were predictable and systematic, allowing the government to budget and plan.

He reformed the currency, issuing new coins with a higher precious metal content. He tried to fix prices through the Edict on Maximum Prices in 301, which set legal maximum prices for hundreds of goods and services. Like most price controls, this didn't work well—people evaded it through black markets—but it showed Diocletian's ambition to restore economic order.

He reformed the army, increasing its size to perhaps 400,000 to 600,000 men and reorganizing it into mobile field armies and permanent frontier garrisons. The field armies could respond quickly to invasions while frontier garrisons held defensive positions.

Diocletian also changed the nature of imperial power. He abandoned the Augustan fiction of being "first citizen" and embraced open autocracy. He styled himself *dominus et deus* ("lord and god"). He surrounded himself with elaborate Persian-style court ceremonies. Subjects prostrated themselves before him. He wore purple silk and jeweled crowns. The emperor was now explicitly an absolute monarch, not a magistrate.

This wasn't megalomania; it was strategic. By emphasizing the emperor's sacred status and surrounding him with ceremony, Diocletian made imperial power seem beyond ordinary reach. You don't casually murder someone who was semi-divine.

Diocletian's reforms worked, as the empire stabilized. But in 305, Diocletian did something unprecedented: he voluntarily retired. He forced Maximian to retire as well. Both Augusti stepped down on the same day. The Caesars became Augusti, new Caesars were appointed, and the Tetrarchy's succession plan was activated.

But it immediately collapsed. Within a year, multiple claimants were fighting for power. The Caesars weren't willing to wait their turn. Biological sons of emperors demanded power.

One of those sons was Constantine. His father Constantius Chlorus had been one of Diocletian's Caesars, governing Britain and Gaul. When Constantius died in 306 at York in Britain, his troops proclaimed Constantine emperor. But so did several other generals and their armies. By 312, there were six men claiming to be emperor. The Tetrarchy's elegant succession mechanism had failed.

Constantine spent the next few years fighting rivals for control. In 312, he marched on Rome to confront Maxentius, who controlled Italy. The two armies met at the Milvian Bridge outside Rome on October 28th, 312. According to Christian sources written later, Constantine had a vision before the battle. It was either a cross of light in the sky or a dream in which Christ told him to mark his soldiers' shields with a Christian symbol. Constantine won the battle decisively. Maxentius drowned while fleeing across the bridge.

Constantine attributed his victory to the Christian God. This would change everything.

## The Rise of Christianity: From Persecution to Imperial Religion

Christianity had been growing steadily throughout the empire for three centuries. Despite periodic persecutions, despite being illegal, and despite being despised by many traditional Romans, Christianity spread. By 300

CE, Christians were perhaps 10 percent of the empire's population. They were still a minority, but their numbers were growing.

Why did Christianity grow during Rome's worst crisis? Well, Christianity promised salvation and eternal life to all believers regardless of social status. In a world where everything seemed to be collapsing, this hope was attractive. The traditional Roman religion offered no clear afterlife, no promise of justice, and no explanation for suffering. Christianity offered all of these.

Christian churches provided social networks, charity, and mutual support. When plague struck, Christians cared for the sick—even non-Christians—while many pagans fled their sick relatives. Nursing sick people improved survival rates, so Christian communities often had lower mortality rates than pagan communities during epidemics. When the economic crisis made people desperate, churches provided food, financial assistance to the poor, and support for widows and orphans. Christian communities functioned as mutual aid societies at a time when traditional civic institutions were failing. This charity converted people as much as theology did; when a Christian community feeds you during a famine, you notice.

Christianity explained suffering as temporary, as a test of faith, and as part of God's plan. It gave cosmic meaning to the chaos. The world might be ending, but Christians believed a new, better world would follow, either after death in heaven or after Christ's return to establish God's kingdom on earth. This hope made present suffering bearable. Traditional Roman religion had no good explanation for why the gods would allow the empire to suffer such catastrophes.

Diocletian saw Christianity as a threat. In 303, he launched the Great Persecution, the last and most systematic attempt to destroy Christianity. Churches were destroyed, scriptures burned, and Christians were required to sacrifice to traditional gods or face execution. The persecution lasted about ten years and varied in intensity by region.

The persecution failed. Christianity was too widespread, too organized, and too resilient. Galerius, one of the tetrarchs, issued an edict of toleration in 311 on his deathbed, effectively admitting defeat. Christianity had survived Rome's worst.

Constantine changed everything. After his victory at the Milvian Bridge in 312, which he attributed to the Christian God, Constantine openly embraced Christianity. In 313, he and Licinius (another claimant to imperial power) issued the Edict of Milan, which legalized Christianity and restored confiscated property to churches.

Constantine didn't just tolerate Christianity; he actively promoted it. He funded church construction, including the original St. Peter's Basilica in Rome. He gave Christian clergy tax exemptions and legal privileges. He made Sunday a day of rest. He got involved in theological disputes, convening the Council of Nicaea in 325 to resolve the Arian controversy about Christ's nature.

Why did Constantine embrace Christianity? The sources, which were mostly written by Christian bishops who admired him, say he had a genuine conversion experience. Modern historians debate whether it was sincere religious belief, political calculation (recognizing Christianity's growing power), or both. What's clear is that Constantine's conversion transformed Christianity's status. When the emperor converted to Christianity, the religion became fashionable and politically advantageous. Conversions increased dramatically.

By 380, Emperor Theodosius I made Christianity the official state religion with the Edict of Thessalonica. Pagan worship was increasingly restricted and eventually banned. The empire that had persecuted Christians for centuries became a Christian empire within eighty years.

This religious transformation was as significant as any political or military development. Christianity would shape medieval and modern Europe. The alliance between the Christian Church and the Roman state would define Western civilization for over a thousand years. Constantine's conversion changed the course of history.

The empire survived the Crisis of the Third Century. The reforms of Diocletian and Constantine created a system that worked well enough. The Eastern Roman Empire, which we call the Byzantine Empire today, would continue for another eleven centuries. Even the Western Roman Empire had nearly two more centuries before its final collapse in 476.

Rome had faced its worst crisis and survived. The question was, for how long?

# Chapter 10: The Long Goodbye: How Rome Fell So Slowly You Could Barely Tell It Was Happening

The Roman Empire didn't fall with a dramatic bang. It didn't collapse overnight. Instead, it experienced what might be the slowest, most gradual decline in history. This process was so slow that people living through it might not have realized they were watching the end of an era.

Here's the thing that confuses people about Rome's "fall": the Roman Empire didn't actually fall in many of the ways we usually think. The Eastern Roman Empire–what we call the Byzantine Empire, though they always called themselves Romans–survived for another thousand years after the traditional "fall" date of 476 CE. Constantinople, the Eastern capital, didn't fall until 1453 when the Ottoman Turks conquered it. That's over a millennium of continuous Roman government, law, and culture.

What fell in the 5th century was the Western Roman Empire, the Latin-speaking half centered in Italy. But even that "fall" was more like a slow transformation than a sudden collapse. Germanic kingdoms gradually replaced Roman administration. Roman institutions persisted under barbarian kings. Latin evolved into Romance languages. Roman law continued. Christianity, which Rome had adopted, spread to the barbarians.

So the "fall of Rome" is really the story of how the unified Mediterranean empire became medieval kingdoms in the West and the Byzantine Empire in the East. It was a messy, complicated process that took centuries and didn't feel like the end of the world to most people living through it.

Let's see how it happened.

### Constantine and Constantinople: Moving the Capital East

We left off with Constantine reunifying the empire in 324 after defeating all his rivals in civil wars that followed the collapse of Diocletian's Tetrarchy. Constantine now ruled alone over the entire Roman Empire.

One of Constantine's most consequential decisions was to found a new capital. Rome still mattered symbolically–it was Rome, after all, the Eternal City, home to the Senate and centuries of tradition. But strategically, Rome's location was terrible. It was far from the frontiers where armies fought Persians and Germanic tribes. It was dominated by pagan aristocratic families who resisted Constantine's Christian innovations. The Senate, though politically weak, still represented traditional republican values and the pagan religion that Constantine wanted to move past. Rome was the past; Constantine wanted to build the future.

So in 324, after defeating his last rival, Licinius, Constantine decided to build a new capital on the site of Byzantium, an ancient Greek city on the Bosphorus Strait where Europe meets Asia. The location was perfect. It controlled the strait connecting the Mediterranean to the Black Sea, which was crucial for grain shipments. It was near the wealthy Eastern provinces, the empire's economic powerhouse. It was close to both the Persian and Danube frontiers. And it was highly defensible, as it was surrounded by water on three sides, making it nearly impregnable.

Constantine poured enormous resources into building his new capital. He constructed massive defensive walls that would be expanded in the 5th century into the Theodosian Walls. These triple walls made Constantinople the most heavily fortified city in the world. He built a hippodrome for chariot racing that could seat perhaps 100,000 spectators. Chariot racing was the most popular sport in the Byzantine Empire, and the hippodrome would be the center of political life for centuries. He constructed forums, monumental columns, aqueducts to bring fresh water, palaces for the emperor and government, public baths, and libraries.

And churches. Lots of churches. This would be a Christian capital, the New Rome, deliberately free from associations with paganism and pagan temples. Constantine founded the Church of the Holy Apostles, where he would eventually be buried alongside relics of the apostles, positioning himself as the thirteenth apostle. He founded the original Hagia Sophia (Holy Wisdom), though the famous building that stands today was built two centuries later under Justinian. Constantinople would have hundreds of churches, monasteries, and Christian institutions, making it visibly and unmistakably a Christian city.

Constantine encouraged migration by offering generous incentives. Free grain distributions modeled on Rome's *annona* ensured that poor citizens could eat. Building programs created jobs for craftsmen, laborers, and architects. Constantine established a Senate in Constantinople to rival Rome's, though initially it had lower status. Its members were called *clari* (distinguished), while Rome's senators were *clarissimi* (most distinguished). Within a generation, Constantinople was rivaling Rome in population, perhaps reaching 300,000 to 400,000 residents by mid-century.

The city was formally dedicated on May 11th, 330, as Constantinople (Constantine's City). The founding of Constantinople had profound consequences. It marked a shift in the empire's center of gravity from West to East. The Eastern provinces were wealthier, more urbanized, and more economically dynamic than the West. By moving the capital east, Constantine was acknowledging that the future of the empire was in the East.

Constantine continued promoting Christianity. He funded churches throughout the empire, including the Church of the Holy Sepulchre in Jerusalem (built over what Christians believed was Jesus's tomb) and the original St. Peter's Basilica in Rome. But Constantine didn't abolish paganism. Pagan temples remained open. The traditional religion was still legal and widely practiced. Constantine walked a careful line, promoting Christianity without alienating the empire's pagan majority. This approach allowed Christianity to grow without triggering a religious civil war.

Constantine died in 337, having been baptized on his deathbed (a common practice since baptism washed away sins, and many people wanted to die freshly purified). He had reunified the empire, stabilized the frontiers, promoted Christianity, and founded a new capital that would outlast Rome itself. His sons—Constantine II, Constantius II, and Constans—inherited the empire and promptly started fighting each other because Roman politics never stayed peaceful for long.

The next fifty years saw the usual pattern of civil wars, usurpations, and brief reigns. However, two developments were particularly significant.

In 361, Constantine's nephew, Julian the Apostate, became emperor and tried to reverse Christianization. Julian was a devoted pagan who wanted to restore the traditional religion. He withdrew Christian privileges, promoted pagan worship, and tried to revive paganism intellectually and culturally. But Julian died in 363 after reigning for only two years; he was killed during a campaign against Persia. His pagan revival died with him, showing that Christianity's growth was irreversible.

The emperor who made Christianity official was Theodosius I. In 380, Theodosius issued the Edict of Thessalonica, declaring that all subjects must follow the Nicene Christian faith. This made Christianity the official state religion. Theodosius went further, banning pagan worship, closing temples, and suppressing pagan practices. By the 390s, being pagan was illegal. The Roman Empire was now officially Christian.

When Theodosius died in 395, he divided the empire between his sons. Arcadius got the East, and Honorius got the West. This division was meant to be administrative, not permanent; both were theoretically part of one empire. But in practice, the division became permanent. The Eastern and Western Roman Empires would develop separately, face different challenges, and have dramatically different fates.

### The Barbarian Invasions: Why They Were Moving In

The term "barbarian invasions" is somewhat misleading. What happened in the 4th and 5th centuries was a complex mix of mass migration (entire peoples moving with families and possessions), military conquest (armed groups seizing territory), and political coercion (using military threats to extract land grants).

Why were these people groups migrating? Northern Europe might have experienced cooler, wetter conditions in the 4th and 5th centuries that made agriculture harder, creating food shortages and pressure for farmable land, though other factors were probably more important. Germanic populations had been growing for centuries. More people meant more land was needed to settle, and the territories beyond Rome's frontiers were filling up. At the same time, Germanic societies were becoming more organized. Successful war leaders were creating tribal confederations, such as the Goths, Alemanni, and Franks, which could mobilize larger forces and undertake ambitious migrations.

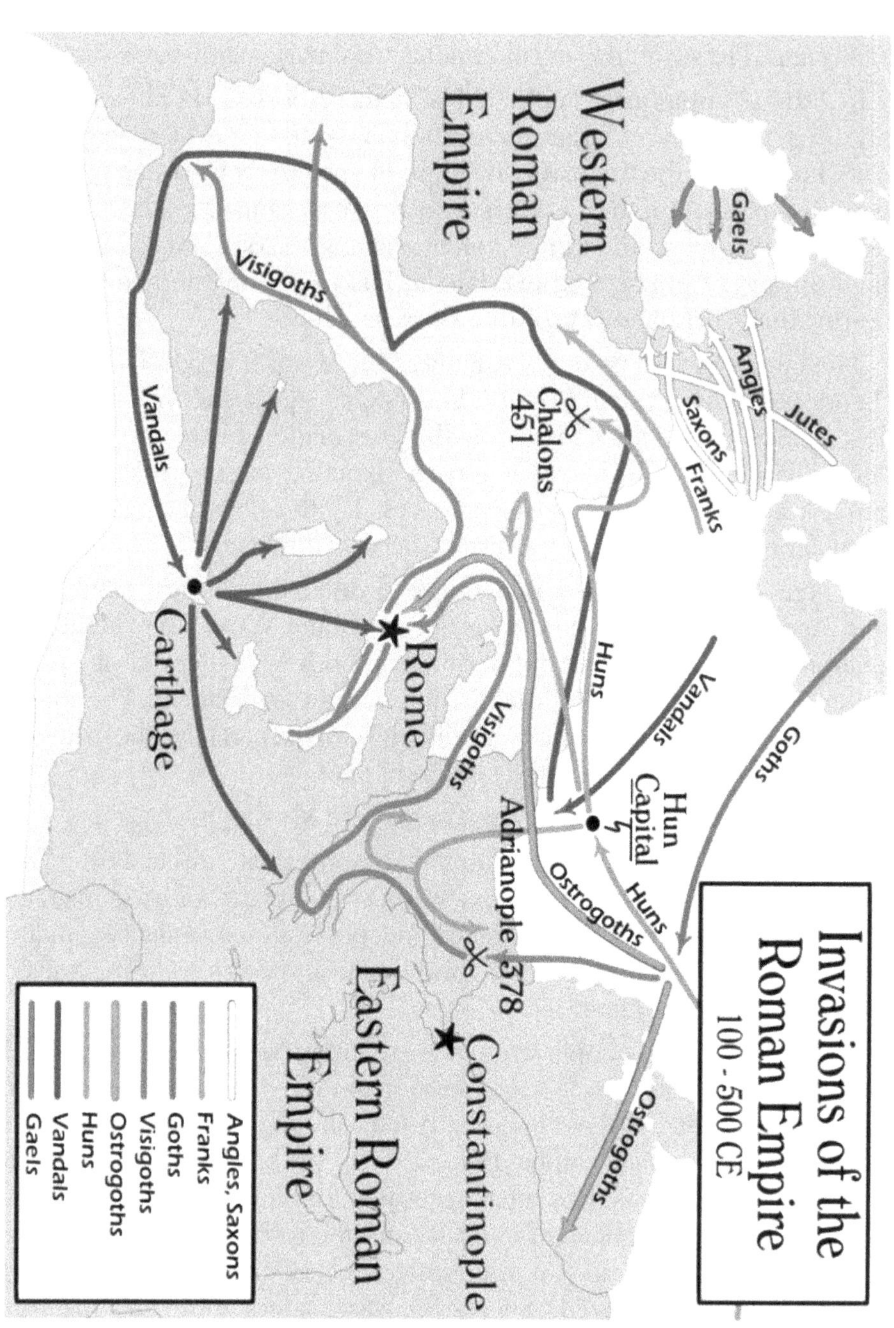


Invasions of the Roman Empire.[27]

Rome's weakness was obvious. The Crisis of the Third Century had shown that Rome could be defeated. Germanic tribes knew that Rome was vulnerable and that the empire's wealth was attractive. Why live in Germania's forests when you could settle in Gaul with its cities, roads, and villas?

However, the immediate trigger was the Huns.

The Huns were a nomadic confederation from the Eurasian Steppe who swept into Europe in the 370s CE. They were formidable warriors. These skilled horsemen used composite bows from horseback with devastating effect. Roman sources describe them as living on horseback and eating raw meat, things that were utterly alien to Roman culture. Modern historians realize these descriptions were stereotypes and exaggerated, but the Huns were certainly militarily effective. They conquered or displaced Germanic tribes in their path, creating a domino effect. Tribes along the Danube and in Ukraine suddenly needed to move—and quickly.

The Huns weren't trying to conquer Rome initially. They were pushing westward, conquering and incorporating Germanic tribes into their confederation, extracting tribute, and building what would become a nomadic empire under Attila in the 440s. But their movement displaced everyone else. Germanic tribes that had been Rome's neighbors for centuries suddenly became desperate refugees seeking safety within Roman borders.

The result was that multiple Germanic peoples appeared at Rome's frontiers in the late 4th and 5th centuries, asking for asylum, demanding land, or simply forcing their way across. The empire faced an unprecedented challenge: how to manage the mass migration of armed populations while defending against other threats.

The Goths provide the clearest example. In 376, a large group of Goths appeared at the Danube frontier asking for asylum. Ancient sources suggest there were perhaps 200,000 people. They were fleeing the Huns and wanted to settle peacefully in Roman territory. Emperor Valens agreed, seeing an opportunity to gain taxpayers and soldiers.

But Roman officials exploited and mistreated the Gothic refugees. They were charged exorbitant prices for food. Their weapons were supposed to be confiscated, although they often weren't. They were settled in inadequate areas. The Goths grew desperate and angry.

In 378, the Goths rebelled. Emperor Valens marched from Constantinople with an army to suppress them. The two forces met at Adrianople (modern Edirne in Turkey) on August 9th, 378 CE.

The Battle of Adrianople was a catastrophe for Rome. Valens's army was destroyed—perhaps two-thirds were killed, possibly twenty thousand men. Valens himself died in the battle, though accounts vary about how.

This was shocking. Roman armies had lost battles before, but this was different. The Goths weren't trying to raid and leave; they were settled in Roman territory and had destroyed an imperial army. The empire couldn't expel or control them. The Goths were now a permanent presence inside the empire, a semi-autonomous people who acknowledged Roman authority nominally but acted independently.

Theodosius I eventually made peace with the Goths in 382, granting them lands in the Balkans in exchange for military service. This seemed like a solution, but it created a precedent. Barbarian peoples could settle inside the empire, maintain their own leadership and identity, and provide soldiers rather than being assimilated into Roman culture.

Over the next decades, more Germanic peoples entered the empire: Vandals, Burgundians, Alans, and Suevi, among others. Some entered peacefully as *foederati* (federated allies), settling in specific areas and providing troops in exchange for land. Others entered violently, fighting Roman armies and carving out territories.

The Western Empire was becoming a patchwork of barbarian-settled regions nominally under Roman authority but practically autonomous. Roman emperors increasingly relied on barbarian generals and troops. Many top military positions were held by men of Germanic origin. The line between "Roman" and "barbarian" was blurring.

### 410 CE: The Sack of Rome—When the Unthinkable Happened

Then came the psychological shock that told everyone the empire was dying: Rome was sacked.

The Visigoths (Western Goths) had settled in the Balkans after 382, providing soldiers for Rome. But they were mistreated, underpaid, and exploited by Roman officials. Their leader, Alaric, demanded better treatment, fair pay, and a proper place in the Roman hierarchy. When the Western Roman government refused, Alaric marched his army into Italy.

The Western Emperor Honorius had moved the capital from Rome to Ravenna, a city on Italy's northeast coast surrounded by marshes. It was easier to defend than Rome. Honorius stayed safe in Ravenna while Alaric besieged Rome three times between 408 and 410.

The third siege succeeded. On August 24th, 410, Alaric's forces entered Rome. What followed was three days of looting, destruction, and violence. However, it was relatively restrained by ancient standards. Alaric was a Christian and ordered his troops not to harm people seeking refuge in churches or to burn the city. Most of Rome's population survived. Still, the symbolism was devastating.

**The Sack of Rome in 410 by the Vandals by Joseph-Noël Sylvestre.**[28]

Rome hadn't been captured by foreign enemies in eight hundred years, not since the Gauls had sacked it in 390 BCE. Rome was supposed to be eternal and protected by the gods. If Rome could fall, nothing was safe.

The psychological impact was profound. Saint Jerome, writing from Bethlehem, said, "The city which had taken the whole world was itself taken." Saint Augustine began writing *The City of God* partly to address the question. If Rome was Christian and protected by God, why did God allow Rome to be sacked?

The sack didn't destroy Rome or end the empire. Alaric withdrew from Rome after three days; he didn't want to rule it, just to pressure the imperial government. He died later that year. The Western Roman Empire continued. Life went on.

### The Long Decline: How the West Slowly Stopped Being Roman

After 410 CE, the Western Empire entered a slow decline. It wasn't dramatic. There was no final catastrophic battle. Instead, the empire gradually lost control over its territories as Germanic kingdoms established themselves on former Roman lands.

Real power in the Western Empire increasingly belonged to military strongmen, usually of Germanic origin. Flavius Aetius, a Roman general, defended what remained of the empire in the 430s and 440s, defeating Attila the Hun's invasion of Gaul in 451 at the Battle of the Catalaunian Plains (with help from Gothic and Frankish allies). But Aetius was murdered in 454 by Emperor Valentinian III, who was then murdered in 455 by Aetius's supporters. The cycle of violence and instability continued.

The Western emperors became increasingly irrelevant. They were proclaimed by military strongmen, recognized or ignored by Constantinople, and held little actual power. Real authority belonged to Germanic generals who commanded the armies, such as Ricimer, Gundobad, and Odoacer.

These Germanic kingdoms didn't destroy the Roman civilization. They tried to preserve it. Germanic kings wanted to rule as Romans did, using Roman law, administration, and legitimacy. They saw themselves as part of the Roman world, not destroyers of it.

In Britain, Roman legions withdrew around 410 to defend more critical areas, particularly Gaul and Italy. Britain was left to defend itself against raiders from Ireland, Scotland, and Germania. The Romano-British population tried to maintain Roman civilization, but without imperial support, Roman institutions gradually collapsed. Within decades, Anglo-Saxon invaders from northern Germany and Denmark were conquering and settling Britain. Unlike other Germanic groups, the Anglo-Saxons largely displaced Romano-British culture rather than assimilating into it. Roman cities were abandoned, villa estates fell into ruin, and Latin ceased to be spoken except by the clergy. By 450, Britain was transitioning from Roman to Anglo-Saxon, though Romano-British culture persisted in Wales, Cornwall, and other western areas. The memory of Roman Britain would later inspire the Arthurian legends—stories of a lost golden age when Britain was civilized and unified.

The situation in Gaul was very different. The Visigoths settled in southwestern Gaul (modern Aquitaine and southern France) after leaving Italy in 412 CE, establishing a kingdom centered in Toulouse. The Burgundians settled in southeastern Gaul (roughly modern Burgundy). The Franks gradually conquered northern Gaul from their base in what's now Belgium and northern France. These Germanic kingdoms maintained Roman structures. Visigothic kings issued laws in Latin based on Roman legal principles; for example, the Visigothic Code combined Germanic customs with Roman law. They employed Roman administrators who knew how to collect taxes and run the government. They preserved cities, though these were not as large as they had been. Latin remained the language of government, law, and religion, though Germanic languages were spoken by the ruling elite.

The Frankish Kingdom under the Merovingian dynasty would prove especially successful. When Clovis, King of the Franks, converted to Catholic Christianity (rather than Arian Christianity that most Germanic tribes practiced) around 496, he gained the support of the Roman Catholic Church and the Gallo-Roman population. The Franks would eventually unite most of Gaul under their rule, preserving Roman law, Latin language, and Christian culture while adding Germanic elements. Frankish Gaul would evolve into medieval France; the name "France" derives from "Franks."

The Visigoths moved from Gaul to Spain in the 470s after being pushed out by the Franks. They established a kingdom centered in Toledo that would last until the Muslim conquest in 711. The Visigothic Kingdom of Spain was highly Romanized. Laws were based on Roman codes, administration followed Roman models, the population remained largely Latin-speaking, and the kings saw themselves as successors to

Roman authority. The Visigoths were a small minority ruling a larger Roman population, so assimilation to Roman culture was a necessity.

In North Africa, the Vandals, led by King Gaiseric, crossed from Spain to North Africa in 429. By 439, they had captured Carthage, one of the empire's most important cities and the center of North Africa's agricultural production. The loss of Africa was economically catastrophic for the Western Empire, as Italy depended heavily on African grain. Without African grain shipments, feeding Italy became a problem that the Western government couldn't solve.

The Vandals established a maritime kingdom based on Carthage's naval power. They built a fleet and raided throughout the Mediterranean. In 455, a Vandal fleet sailed to Rome and sacked it more thoroughly than Alaric's Visigoths had in 410, though still without massive slaughter. The Vandals ruled North Africa using Roman administrative systems, collected taxes as Romans had, and maintained the agricultural estates that produced grain and olive oil.

Italy itself remained nominally under Western Roman control until 476, but real power lay with Germanic generals who commanded the armies. Odoacer, who deposed the last Western emperor, governed Italy as "King of Italy" using entirely Roman systems. He maintained the Senate, Roman law, tax collection, and administration. For the Roman population of Italy, Odoacer's rule didn't feel dramatically different from having a weak Roman emperor, which was what they'd had for decades anyway.

In 493, the Ostrogoths (Eastern Goths) under Theodoric conquered Italy. Theodoric ruled as king of Italy from 493 to 526, and his reign was remarkably successful. He preserved Roman institutions, employed Roman senators in government, patronized Roman culture, and saw himself as continuing the Roman imperial tradition. Theodoric's court at Ravenna patronized scholars, preserved Latin literature, and maintained classical education. The Roman population viewed Theodoric as a legitimate ruler, and his kingdom was stable and prosperous.

By 500 CE, the Western Roman Empire no longer existed as a political entity. However, former Roman territories were ruled by Germanic kingdoms that preserved Roman law, the Latin language, Christianity, and much of Roman civilization.

## 476 CE: The End That Wasn't Really an End

In 475 CE, a general named Orestes made his young son emperor. The boy's name was Romulus Augustulus, ironically named after Rome's legendary founder, Romulus, and its first emperor, Augustus. He was between twelve and sixteen years old.

Romulus Augustulus had no real power. He was a puppet emperor installed by his father. He ruled from Ravenna, not Rome. He controlled barely any territory beyond Italy. He was emperor in name only.

In 476, Germanic soldiers in Italy demanded land. When Orestes refused, the soldiers mutinied. They proclaimed their commander, Odoacer, as king. Odoacer's forces captured Ravenna, and Orestes was executed. Romulus Augustulus was deposed.

But Odoacer didn't proclaim himself emperor. He didn't need to. Instead, he sent the imperial regalia—the crown, purple robes, and other symbols of the imperial office—to Constantinople. He informed Emperor Zeno that the West didn't need its own emperor. The Eastern emperor could rule the whole empire in theory. Odoacer would govern Italy as his representative, holding the title "King of Italy."

Zeno accepted this arrangement, though he also recognized Julius Nepos (a previous Western emperor living in exile) as the legitimate Western emperor. When Nepos died in 480, Zeno didn't appoint a replacement. The Western Roman Empire had ended, not through dramatic conquest but through administrative adjustment.

This is why 476 CE is traditionally marked as the "fall of Rome." The last Western emperor had been deposed. The Western imperial office ceased to exist. However, nothing dramatic happened on the ground. The city of Rome continued to stand.

For most people in Italy, daily life didn't change. They had a king instead of an emperor, but he governed through existing institutions. They still paid taxes, still went to church, and still spoke Latin. Rome had "fallen," but most Romans barely noticed.

## What Caused the Fall? (Every Historian Has a Theory)

Historians have been arguing about why Rome fell for over 1,500 years. Edward Gibbon's *The Decline and Fall of the Roman Empire* (1776-1789) blamed Christianity for sapping Roman military virtue. Other theories have blamed:

- Barbarian invasions
- Economic decline
- Moral decay
- Government corruption
- Military weakness
- Division of the empire
- Loss of civic virtue
- Climate change
- Plague
- Currency debasement
- Overextension
- Bad emperors
- Christianity (for weakening traditional values)
- Paganism (for angering the Christian God)

Modern historians believe the fall was caused by many interacting factors rather than one single thing.

Economically, the Western Roman Empire was weaker than the East. It had fewer wealthy cities, less developed trade, and a more vulnerable tax base. When territories were lost to Germanic kingdoms, tax revenue collapsed. The government couldn't afford to pay soldiers. Unpaid soldiers became unreliable or rebelled.

Militarily, the army became increasingly composed of barbarian foederati whose loyalty lay with their tribal leaders, not with Rome. When conflicts arose, these troops often fought for barbarian interests rather than Roman ones. The empire depended on barbarians to defend against other barbarians, which was an unstable situation.

Politically, the Western government lacked legitimacy and effectiveness. Emperors were frequently children controlled by generals. Real power belonged to military strongmen. The government couldn't command loyalty or enforce its will. Political fragmentation was severe.

Demographically, plague and warfare had reduced the empire's population. Fewer people meant fewer taxpayers and fewer potential soldiers. Some regions never recovered their pre-crisis populations.

Geopolitically, the West faced greater external pressure than the East. Germanic migrations affected the Rhine and Danube frontiers, the West's borders. The East faced Persian threats but managed them better and could use diplomacy and gold to deflect barbarian pressure toward the West.

Some historians argue we shouldn't call it a "fall" at all. The Western Empire transformed into Germanic kingdoms that preserved Roman law, Christianity, the Latin language (evolving into Romance languages), and many Roman institutions. Roman civilization didn't end; it evolved into medieval European civilization.

The truth is, Rome probably fell because empires fall. All political structures are temporary. Rome lasted longer than most—over one thousand years from the republic to the fall of the West and over two thousand years if you count the Byzantine Empire. That's an extraordinary run. What's remarkable isn't that Rome fell, but that it lasted so long.

### The Byzantine Survivor: Why the East Lived On

While the West fragmented into Germanic kingdoms, the Eastern Roman Empire thrived. Why?

The East was simply wealthier. Cities like Constantinople, Alexandria, Antioch, and Ephesus were major economic centers. Trade routes connected the East to Asia, bringing in spices, silk, and luxury goods. Tax revenues were higher and more reliable. Geography helped too; Constantinople was nearly impregnable, surrounded by water with massive land walls. The Danube frontier was shorter and easier to defend than the Rhine-Danube line the West had to protect.

Eastern emperors were masterful diplomats. They played barbarian tribes against each other, paid to redirect barbarian attacks toward the West, and used marriage alliances, religious conversion, and political manipulation to manage threats without always fighting. The Eastern government remained functional in ways the West's didn't. It could collect taxes, pay soldiers, maintain infrastructure, and enforce laws. The bureaucracy worked. This sounds basic, but it's important—states survive when their governments can govern.

The Eastern army remained professional, well paid, and loyal. It could defend frontiers, suppress rebellions, and respond to crises. Unlike the West, the East didn't rely heavily on barbarian foederati whose loyalty was questionable. The East was also more culturally unified. Greek was the common language of administration, commerce, and culture, though many local languages persisted. Orthodox Christianity provided religious unity and cultural identity. There was a sense of shared identity as Romans (*Romaioi* in Greek), even as the empire became increasingly Greek in language and culture while preserving Roman political and legal traditions.

The Byzantine Empire would face enormous challenges over the next millennium, but it would repeatedly demonstrate remarkable resilience. Emperor Justinian I (r. 527–565 CE) temporarily reconquered much of the former Western Empire. His general Belisarius defeated the Vandals in North Africa (533–534 CE) and conquered the Ostrogothic Kingdom in Italy (535–554 CE), though the Italian conquest was devastating and took twenty years of brutal warfare. Justinian's forces also reconquered parts of southern Spain.

For a brief period, the Mediterranean was Roman again. But Justinian's reconquests were expensive and temporary. The empire couldn't hold these western territories permanently. After Justinian's death, the Lombards invaded Italy in 568, conquering much of it and leaving Byzantium with only scattered holdings. The effort to reconquer the West had stretched Byzantine resources dangerously thin.

Justinian's more lasting achievement was codifying Roman law. The *Corpus Juris Civilis* (Body of Civil Law) systematized centuries of Roman legal tradition. It remains the foundation of civil-law systems throughout Europe and Latin America today. Justinian also built the magnificent Hagia Sophia in Constantinople, an architectural marvel with its massive dome that seemed to float on light. It stood as Christendom's greatest church for nine hundred years.

In the 6th and 7th centuries, Byzantium fought endless wars with the Sasanian Persian Empire. These conflicts drained both empires' resources in wars of attrition that neither could definitively win. The Byzantine-Persian Wars reached their climax between 602 and 628 CE, when the Persians conquered Syria, Palestine, Egypt, and parts of Anatolia. These devastating losses seemed to herald Byzantium's end. But Emperor Heraclius (r. 610–641 CE) fought back, defeated the Persians, and recovered the lost territories by 628.

Both Byzantium and Persia were exhausted by their long wars. Then a new force emerged: Islam. Arab armies erupted from Arabia in the 630s, conquering with stunning speed. By 650, the Arabs had conquered Syria, Palestine, Egypt, Mesopotamia, and Persia. The Byzantine Empire lost its wealthiest provinces. The loss of Egypt was particularly devastating economically. But Byzantium survived. Constantinople's walls held against multiple Arab sieges, most famously in 678 CE and 718. Byzantine forces used Greek fire, an incendiary weapon whose exact composition remains unknown, to destroy Arab fleets. The empire contracted to Anatolia, the Balkans, and scattered holdings, but the core survived and eventually stabilized.

Under the Macedonian dynasty in the 9th through 11th centuries, Byzantium experienced a cultural and military revival. Byzantine forces reconquered territories from the Arabs. The economy recovered. Constantinople became one of the world's greatest cities. It had perhaps 400,000 inhabitants and was wealthy, sophisticated, and a center of trade between Asia and Europe. Byzantine culture flourished. This was Byzantium's golden age. It was Christianity's strongest defender and Mediterranean civilization's greatest power.

Byzantium's decline came not from Muslims but from fellow Christians. The Fourth Crusade, intended to fight Muslims in Egypt, instead attacked Constantinople in 1204. Crusaders sacked the city, massacring civilians, looting treasures, and destroying irreplaceable manuscripts and art. They established the Latin Empire of Constantinople while Byzantine refugees established competing states. Byzantine forces recaptured Constantinople in 1261 under Michael VIII Palaiologos, but the empire was shattered. It never recovered its former strength. Over the next two centuries, the Ottoman Turks conquered Byzantine territories piece by piece.

By the 1450s, the Byzantine Empire consisted of little more than Constantinople and its immediate surroundings. Sultan Mehmed II of the Ottoman Empire besieged Constantinople in April 1453 with a huge army and massive cannons capable of breaching the ancient walls. After nearly two months, on May 29th, 1453, Ottoman forces breached the walls and took the city. Emperor Constantine XI died fighting in the streets. The Byzantine Empire ended.

The Byzantine Empire had lasted over one thousand years from Constantine's founding of Constantinople to its fall to the Ottomans. During that millennium, it preserved Roman law, Greek philosophy, and Christian theology. It served as a buffer protecting Europe from successive waves of invaders. It spread classical learning to medieval Europe and the Islamic world. When Constantinople fell, Byzantine scholars fled to Italy, bringing manuscripts and knowledge that helped spark the Renaissance.

The Byzantine Empire was the Roman Empire. Its citizens called themselves Romans (*Romaioi* in Greek). Its emperors claimed to be the legitimate successors of Augustus. Its laws were based on Justinian's codification of Roman law. When it finally fell in 1453, the Roman Empire truly ended.

# Conclusion: The Eternal City

We started this journey in 753 BCE, with Romulus drawing a plow around Palatine Hill. We watched Rome grow from a village into a republic, transform into an empire ruling lands from Britain to Mesopotamia, survive catastrophic crises, and finally—slowly, messily—transform into the medieval world.

Did Rome fall? Yes and no.

The Western Empire collapsed in the 5th century CE. The Eastern Empire survived another thousand years, until 1453. But Rome's legacy never died.

## What Rome Left Behind

Modern legal systems throughout Europe, Latin America, and much of the world are based on Roman law. Concepts like contracts, property rights, legal procedure, and civil law all trace back to Rome. Latin did not die; it evolved into French, Spanish, Italian, Portuguese, and Romanian. English, though Germanic, borrowed thousands of Latin words. Latin still appears in legal, medical, and scientific terminology.

The religion Rome adopted shaped Western civilization for nearly two thousand years. The organizational structure of the Catholic Church mirrors that of the Roman imperial administration. The alliance between church and state that Constantine forged influenced medieval and modern politics. Roman roads still serve as foundations for modern highways. Roman engineering principles—the arch, the vault, and concrete—

influenced architecture for centuries. Aqueducts, bridges, and buildings that the Romans built still stand.

The idea of a universal empire ruling diverse peoples under a common law endured long after Rome's political power faded. The Holy Roman Empire, the Russian concept of a "Third Rome," and even modern global powers have been compared to Rome. Roman writers, such as Cicero, Virgil, Ovid, Seneca, and Marcus Aurelius, shaped Western literature and thought. Renaissance humanists looked to Rome for models of eloquence and virtue. Enlightenment thinkers drew on Roman republican ideals. Rome pioneered the idea that citizenship was a legal status with defined rights and obligations, separate from ethnicity or birthplace; this revolutionary concept influenced modern ideas of citizenship and democracy.

When we say "Western civilization," what we mostly refer to is Roman civilization that has been transformed through the centuries.

### What We Can Learn from Rome's Rise and Fall

Rome lasted over a thousand years, from the Roman Republic's establishment to the Western Empire's end–or more than two thousand years if Byzantium is included. By any measure, that was extraordinary. What made Rome successful, and what finally brought it down?

Rome's success came from pragmatism over ideology. Rome adapted constantly, borrowing from Greeks, Etruscans, and Carthaginians. It granted citizenship to former enemies and assimilated conquered peoples rather than merely exploiting them. Flexibility kept Rome relevant as circumstances changed.

Rome survived bad emperors when its institutions–the army, the bureaucracy, and the legal system–functioned independently. Good systems can withstand poor leadership, at least temporarily. Roads, aqueducts, and ports were not just engineering feats; they made an empire possible. Moving armies, goods, and ideas quickly created economic and political integration.

But Rome's failures are equally instructive. Rome conquered more territory than it could sustainably govern or defend. The frontiers became indefensible, resources were stretched too thin, and size became a liability. The gap between the rich and the poor destroyed the republic. When wealth was concentrated in a few hands, when the middle class disappeared, and when the masses depended on handouts, stability collapsed. Economic inequality bred political instability.

When Rome relied on barbarian soldiers to defend against barbarians, when generals became kingmakers, and when armies murdered emperors for better pay, military force replaced legitimacy. Once violence became the path to power, violence became constant. When governments inflated currency to pay their bills, they destroyed economic trust. Rome's 3rd-century hyperinflation devastated the economy and took generations to recover.

These are not just ancient problems. Modern societies face similar questions. How do you govern complex, diverse populations? How do you balance security and freedom? How do you prevent inequality from destroying political stability? How do you maintain institutions when individuals seek power? How do you know when you have overextended?

Rome had no easy answers. Neither do we.

### The Final Word

Rome was brutal and brilliant, generous and cruel, sophisticated and savage. It was built on slavery and conquest, but also on law and engineering. It gave us philosophy, gladiatorial combat, aqueducts, and crucifixions.

Rome was never one thing. It was a republic and an empire, pagan and Christian, Italian and multicultural. It conquered through violence and won loyalty through citizenship. It collapsed in the West and endured in the East, or perhaps it simply transformed into something new.

Understanding Rome means understanding contradiction—how the same civilization produced both *Meditations* and bloodsports, both sophisticated law and casual brutality.

But most importantly, understanding Rome means understanding that we are still shaped by it. Our institutions, our languages, our laws, and our cities are all Roman inheritances. When we struggle with how to govern diverse populations, balance security and freedom, or create lasting institutions, we face the same challenges Rome faced.

Rome taught us that empires are temporary but that ideas endure. Rome's political power ended long ago, but Roman law, language, architecture, and political concepts still shape the world. What matters is not how long power lasts, but what it leaves behind.

Rome's story is not just about the past. It is about us.

## Here's another book by Matt Clayton that you might like

# Free Bonus from Captivating History (Available for a Limited time)

Hi History Lovers!

Now you have a chance to join our exclusive history list so you can get your first history ebook for free as well as discounts and a potential to get more history books for free!

Simply visit the link below to join.

captivatinghistory.com/ebook

Or, Scan the QR code!

Also, make sure to follow us on Facebook, X, and YouTube by searching for Captivating History.

# References

Beard, Mary. *SPQR: A History of Ancient Rome*. New York: Liveright Publishing, 2015.

Caesar, Julius. *The Gallic War*. Translated by Carolyn Hammond. Oxford: Oxford University Press, 1996.

Cornell, T. J. *The Beginnings of Rome: Italy and Rome from the Bronze Age to the Punic Wars (c. 1000–264 BC)*. London: Routledge, 1995.

Eck, Werner. *The Age of Augustus*. 2nd ed. Translated by Deborah Lucas Schneider. Oxford: Blackwell, 2007.

Everitt, Anthony. *Augustus: The Life of Rome's First Emperor*. New York: Random House, 2006.

Forsythe, Gary. *A Critical History of Early Rome: From Prehistory to the First Punic War*. Berkeley: University of California Press, 2005.

Garnsey, Peter, and Richard Saller. *The Roman Empire: Economy, Society and Culture*. 2nd ed. Oakland: University of California Press, 2014.

Gelzer, Matthias. *Caesar: Politician and Statesman*. Translated by Peter Needham. Cambridge, MA: Harvard University Press, 1968.

Goldsworthy, Adrian. *Augustus: First Emperor of Rome*. New Haven: Yale University Press, 2014.

Goldsworthy, Adrian. *Caesar: Life of a Colossus*. New Haven: Yale University Press, 2006.

Goldsworthy, Adrian. *The Complete Roman Army*. London: Thames & Hudson, 2003.

Goldsworthy, Adrian. *The Punic Wars*. London: Cassell, 2000.

Gruen, Erich S. "The Making of the Principate." In *The Cambridge Ancient History*, vol. 10, 2nd ed., 70–96. Cambridge: Cambridge University Press, 1996.

Halsall, Guy. *Barbarian Migrations and the Roman West, 376–568.* Cambridge: Cambridge University Press, 2007.

Heather, Peter. *The Fall of the Roman Empire: A New History of Rome and the Barbarians.* Oxford: Oxford University Press, 2006.

Hoyos, Dexter. *Mastering the West: Rome and Carthage at War.* Oxford: Oxford University Press, 2015.

Kulikowski, Michael. *Imperial Tragedy: From Constantine's Empire to the Destruction of Roman Italy, AD 363–568.* London: Profile Books, 2019.

Lancel, Serge. *Carthage: A History.* Translated by Antonia Nevill. Oxford: Blackwell, 1995.

Lazenby, J. F. *Hannibal's War: A Military History of the Second Punic War.* Norman: University of Oklahoma Press, 1998.

Livy. *The Early History of Rome (Books I–V of The History of Rome from Its Foundation).* Translated by Aubrey de Sélincourt. London: Penguin Classics, 2002.

Livy. *The War with Hannibal (Books XXI–XXX of The History of Rome from Its Foundation).* Translated by Aubrey de Sélincourt. London: Penguin Classics, 1972.

Meier, Christian. *Caesar: A Biography.* Translated by David McLintock. New York: Basic Books, 1995.

Millar, Fergus. *The Roman Republic in Political Thought.* Hanover, NH: University Press of New England, 2002.

Mitchell, Stephen. *A History of the Later Roman Empire, AD 284–641.* 2nd ed. Oxford: Wiley-Blackwell, 2015.

Osgood, Josiah. *Caesar's Legacy: Civil War and the Emergence of the Roman Empire.* Cambridge: Cambridge University Press, 2006.

Plutarch. *Life of Caesar.* In *Fall of the Roman Republic.* Translated by Rex Warner. London: Penguin Classics, 1972.

Polybius. *The Histories.* Translated by Robin Waterfield. Oxford: Oxford University Press, 2010.

Scullard, H. H. *Scipio Africanus: Soldier and Politician.* Ithaca, NY: Cornell University Press, 1970.

Smith, Christopher. *Early Rome and Latium: Economy and Society c. 1000 to 500 BC.* Oxford: Clarendon Press, 1996.

Southern, Pat. *Augustus.* 2nd ed. London: Routledge, 2014.

Strauss, Barry. *The Death of Caesar: The Story of History's Most Famous Assassination.* New York: Simon & Schuster, 2015.

Suetonius. *The Twelve Caesars.* Translated by Robert Graves. London: Penguin Classics, 2007.

Syme, Ronald. *The Roman Revolution.* Oxford: Oxford University Press, 1939.

Ward-Perkins, Bryan. *The Fall of Rome and the End of Civilization.* Oxford: Oxford University Press, 2005.

Wickham, Chris. *The Inheritance of Rome: Illuminating the Dark Ages, 400-1000.* New York: Penguin, 2009.

# Image Sources

1 Capitoline Museums, CC0, via Wikimedia Commons, https://commons.wikimedia.org/wiki/File:Lupa_Capitolina,_Rome.jpg

2 Renata3, CC BY-SA 4.0 <https://creativecommons.org/licenses/by-sa/4.0>, via Wikimedia Commons, https://commons.wikimedia.org/wiki/File: Seven_Hills_of_Rome.svg

3 Abduction of a Sabine Woman (1579–1583), by Giambologna, https://commons.wikimedia.org/wiki/File:Giambologna_sabine.jpg

4 BeBo86, CC BY-SA 3.0 <https://creativecommons.org/licenses/by-sa/3.0>, via Wikimedia Commons, https://commons.wikimedia.org/wiki/File: Forum_romanum_6k_(5760x2097).jpg

5 https://commons.wikimedia.org/wiki/File:Danseurs_et_musiciens,_tombe_des_l%C3%A9opards.jpg

6 Harrias, CC BY-SA 4.0 <https://creativecommons.org/licenses/by-sa/4.0>, via Wikimedia Commons, https://commons.wikimedia.org/wiki/ File:First_Punic_War_264_BC_v3.png

7 William Robert Shepherd, CC BY-SA 4.0 <https://creativecommons.org/licenses/by-sa/4.0>, via Wikimedia Commons, https://commons.wikimedia.org/wiki/File:Map_of_Rome_and_Carthage_at_the_start_of_the_Second_Punic_War_Modified.svg

8 Harrias, CC BY 3.0 <https://creativecommons.org/licenses/by/3.0>, via Wikimedia Commons, https://commons.wikimedia.org/wiki/File:Publius_Scipio%27s_Invasion_of_Africa,_204%E2%80%93201_BC.png

9 Classical Numismatic Group, Inc. http://www.cngcoins.com, CC BY-SA 2.5 <https://creativecommons.org/licenses/by-sa/2.5>, via Wikimedia Commons,

https://commons.wikimedia.org/wiki/File:Q._Pompeius_Rufus,_denarius,_54_BC,_RRC_434-1_(Sulla_only).jpg

10 https://commons.wikimedia.org/wiki/File:Landing_of_the_Romans_on_the_Coast_of_Kent.jpg

11 https://commons.wikimedia.org/wiki/File:Retrato_de_Julio_C%C3%A9sar_(26724093101)_(cropped).jpg

12 Bust: unknown ancient Roman artist of the 1st century AD; photo: unknown photographer., CC BY-SA 4.0 <https://creativecommons.org/licenses/by-sa/4.0>, via Wikimedia Commons, https://commons.wikimedia.org/wiki/File: Marble_bust_of_Mark_Antony_(Vatican_Museums).jpg

13 Vatican Museums, CC BY-SA 4.0 <https://creativecommons.org/licenses/by-sa/4.0>, via Wikimedia Commons, https://commons.wikimedia.org/wiki/File: Augustus_of_Prima_Porta_(inv._2290).jpg

14 https://commons.wikimedia.org/wiki/File:Cicero_Denounces_Catiline_in_the_Roman_Senate_by_Cesare_Maccari.png

15 Carole Raddato from FRANKFURT, Germany, CC BY-SA 2.0 <https://creativecommons.org/licenses/by-sa/2.0>, via Wikimedia Commons, https://commons.wikimedia.org/wiki/File:Vespasian,_from_Naples,_c._AD_70,_Ny_Carlsberg_Glyptotek,_Copenhagen_(13646730625).jpg

16 FeaturedPics, CC BY-SA 4.0 <https://creativecommons.org/licenses/by-sa/4.0>, via Wikimedia Commons, https://commons.wikimedia.org/wiki/File: Colosseo_2020.jpg

17 TimeTravelRome, CC BY 2.0 <https://creativecommons.org/licenses/by/2.0>, via Wikimedia Commons, https://commons.wikimedia.org/wiki/File: Nennig_Roman_Villa_and_Mosaics_-_51134391753.jpg

18 https://commons.wikimedia.org/wiki/File:Appia_antica_2-7-05_048.jpg

19 Roberto Ferrari, CC BY-SA 2.0 <https://creativecommons.org/licenses/by-sa/2.0>, via Wikimedia Commons, https://commons.wikimedia.org/wiki/File: Pont_du_Gard_3.jpg

20 https://commons.wikimedia.org/wiki/File:Mercati_di_Traiano,_2013.jpg

21 Tataryn77, CC BY-SA 3.0 <https://creativecommons.org/licenses/by-sa/3.0>, via Wikimedia Commons, https://commons.wikimedia.org/wiki/File: RomanEmpireTrajan117AD.png

22 NormanEinstein. This file is licensed under the Creative Commons Attribution-Share Alike 3.0 Unported license, https://creativecommons.org/licenses/by-sa/3.0/deed.en, https://commons.wikimedia.org/wiki/File:Hadrians_Wall_map.png

23 Mohammad Reza Domiri Ganji, CC BY-SA 4.0 <https://creativecommons.org/licenses/by-sa/4.0>, via Wikimedia Commons, https://commons.wikimedia.org/wiki/File:Rome-Pantheon.jpg

24 Capitoline Museums, CC BY 2.0 <https://creativecommons.org/licenses/by/2.0>, via Wikimedia Commons,

https://commons.wikimedia.org/wiki/File:Septimius_Severus_busto-Musei_Capitolini.jpg

25 Blank map of South Europe and North Africa.svg: historicair 23:27, 8 August 2007 (UTC), CC BY-SA 2.5 <https://creativecommons.org/licenses/by-sa/2.5>, via Wikimedia Commons, https://commons.wikimedia.org/wiki/File: Map_of_Ancient_Rome_271_AD.svg

26 https://commons.wikimedia.org/wiki/File:Celio_-_le_mura_tra_porta_san_Sebastiano_e_porta_Ardeatina_1974.JPG

27 User:MapMaster, CC BY-SA 2.5 <https://creativecommons.org/licenses/by-sa/2.5>, via Wikimedia Commons, https://commons.wikimedia.org/wiki/File:Invasions_of_the_Roman_Empire_1.png

28 https://commons.wikimedia.org/wiki/File:Sack_of_Rome_by_the_Visigoths_on_24_August_410_by_JN_Sylvestre_1890.jpg